W9-ALL-700

The Aspiring Poet's Journal

For Annemarie K.

The Aspiring Poet's Journal

Bernard Friot

ILLUSTRATIONS BY Hervé Tullet

Abrams Books for Young Readers
New York

No one can help or counsel you, no one.
There is but one way. Enter into yourself.
Seek out in the furthest depths of yourself
the reason that compels you to write;
see if it extends its roots to the very depths of your heart.

—Rainer Maria Rilke, *Letters to a Young Poet*

Explore, by all means, and begin again—indefinitely.
One could also say: experiment.
Try, exploit, invent, imitate, elaborate . . .
Then go back, analyze, pick up again, modify,
observe, and experience something new.
Attempt all the different styles: discover words' endless possibilities,
diversify your writing movements, embrace language and its sounds,
give yourself rules, but also break them.
Write intelligently, humorously, sentimentally.
First, brush the page with your fingertips, let your gaze linger on the
lines, colors and shapes.
Read, write—out loud, softly.
Alone, or with others. Eventually, find your voice and assert it.
But don't speak too much: act, and be.

—Bernard Friot

A poem begins with a lump in the throat.
—Robert Frost

Let's start by writing. That's right—
write your first poem of the year using
the following words:
write—first—poem—year.
If you need a nudge, read the bottom
of the page.

You can write a "list poem" beginning
with one of these phrases:
In one year . . .
I will give you . . .
A poem for . . .

We may not know what poetry is, but we recognize it
when we see it.
—Jean L'Anselme

What does poetry mean to you?
Give as many definitions as possible.

Poetry is . . .

What would I say to you about poetry?
What would I say about these clouds, about the sky?
Look at them, look at them, look at them . . . and nothing
more. You will understand that a poet can't say anything
about Poetry. Leave that task to the critics and professors.
—Federico Garcia Lorca

Nevertheless, here is what two poets have to say:

Poetry is the spontaneous overflow of powerful feelings: it
takes its origin from emotion recollected in tranquility.
—William Wordsworth

Poetry is what in a poem makes you laugh, cry, prickle, be
silent, makes your toe nails twinkle, makes you want to
do this or that or nothing, makes you know that you are
alone in the unknown world, that your bliss and suffering
is forever shared and forever all your own.
—Dylan Thomas

Day 3

Now it's your turn: What would you say about poetry?

Poetry itself cannot be defined; it is what gives us the
power of definition.
—Adonis

Ask ten people the following question:

What does poetry mean to you?

Poetry is a true account of life.
It's my childhood summed up in several words.

Poetry is terrible.
Poetry is pouring your heart into verse that you hope others will understand.

Poetry is giving meaning to words.

Poetry is for losers!

Poetry is a river beginning to flow. Spring.

Poetry always has an ending.

(These definitions were submitted by sixth-grade students at a middle school in Poligny, France)

A poem should not mean, but be.
—Archibald MacLeish

Here are five different texts: Which ones, in your opinion, are poetry? If you prefer, you can discuss it among friends. Make a note of your reasons and arguments.

1
I embraced the summer dawn.
Nothing yet stirred on the palace facades. The water was dead. Camps of shadows remained on the wooded path. I walked, awakening quick, warm breaths as stones looked on and wings rose without a sound.

2
1
BLACK
gray 22
gray 333
gray 4444
gray 55555
gray 666666
gray 7777777
gray 88888888
∞ white

3
When you are old and grey and full of sleep,
And nodding by the fire, take down this book,
And slowly read, and dream of the soft look
Your eyes had once, and of their shadows deep

4
The sea is calm to-night.
The tide is full, the moon lies fair
Upon the straits; on the French coast the light
Gleams and is gone; the cliffs of England stand;
Glimmering and vast, out in the tranquil bay.

5
How doth the little crocodile
   Improve his shining tail,
And pour the waters of the Nile
   On every golden scale!

Day 5

1. Arthur Rimbaud, excerpts of "Dawn," from *Illuminations*
2. Patrick Beurard-Valdoye, *Theory of Names*
3. William Butler Yeats, excerpt from "When You are Old"
4. Matthew Arnold, excerpt from "Dover Beach"
5. Lewis Carroll, excerpt from "The Crocodile"

They say that poetry is defined by its opposite.
But what is the opposite of poetry?
—Mahmoud Darwish

Poetry isn't . . .

A definition in the inverse:

The opposite of poetry is . . .

Begin compiling an anthology of
your favorite poems, either in a notebook or on your computer. The word
"anthology," by the way, is made up of
two Greek words: *anthos* (flower) and
legein (to gather).

Day 7

What's in a name? That which we call a rose
By any other name would smell as sweet.
—William Shakespeare

Read this old English nursery rhyme:

O Mother, I shall be married
To Mr. Punchinello,
To Mr. Punch,
To Mr. Joe,
To Mr. Nell,
To Mr. Lo,
Mr. Punch, Mr. Joe, Mr. Nell, Mr. Lo,
To Mr. Punchinello.

What kinds of words or sounds do you hear in your first or last name?

The French poet Alain Bosquet wrote a "questionnaire-poem" that begins like this:

Father: marble
Mother: rose
Birthplace: in your depths
Date: a year without a year . . .
Religion: the ocean, when it's calm

Now it's your turn. Respond (poetically) to this questionnaire:

Father:
Mother:
Birthplace:
Date:
Schools:
Address:
Profession:
Religion:
Hobbies:
Identifying Feature:

Day 9

You can, of course, invent your own questionnaire.

Poetry is the autobiography of us all.
Poetry is the autobiography of no one.
—Jacques Roubaud

In silent night when rest I took,
For sorrow near I did not look,
I waken'd was with thundering noise
And piteous shrieks of dreadfull voice.
That fearfull sound of 'Fire!' and 'Fire!'
Let no man know is my Desire.

I, starting up, the light did spye,
And to my God my heart did cry
To strengthen me in my Distresse,
And not to leave me succourless.
Then coming out, beheld apace
The flame consume my dwelling place.

—Anne Bradstreet,
from "Upon the Burning of
our House July 10th, 1666"

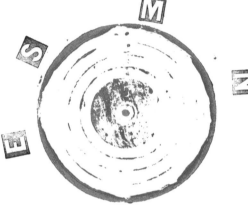

Now write your own autobiographical poem.

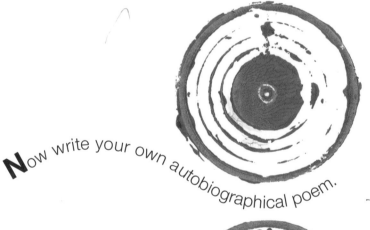

Beginning a poem:
Choose a word—the first that pops into your head. Write it in the middle of a piece of paper. Then, as quickly as you can, jot down any words that you associate with it, making a circle around the original word. In a second circle, write down words that you associate with the words in the first circle. Continue until you've filled up the entire page. Next, pick out two words "geographically" distant from each other on the page and begin writing your poem.

Day 11

The word that I write writes another word on the
other side of the paper.
—Roberto Juarroz

Redo the activity from yesterday.
Go back to your list of associated words
and choose two different words. This
time, write the first word at the top of the
page and the second word on the bottom. Now write a poem that links these
two words.

The Swiss poet Maurice Chappaz explains how he started to write poetry:

> My method for writing poetry was to write a single line, or verse. I would concentrate on that single line and rewrite it while thinking of the next one; I would rewrite it perhaps fifty times over and then all of a sudden, at the fiftieth rewrite, the next verse would come to me. Then I would continue with these two verses, write them over again until the third verse would appear. This is how I wrote, having never written a poem before.

Day 13

Try to apply this method.
To begin, start with this verse from "The Telephone" by Robert Frost:

When I was just as far as I could walk

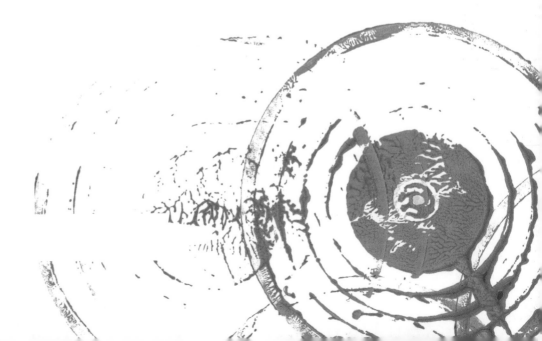

I have never started a poem whose end I knew. Writing
a poem is discovering.
—Robert Frost

Do the same exercise as yesterday, but this time, you write the first verse.

To be worthy of his tree, a poet must prove that he is
both its bark and its root.
—Alain Bosquet

Charles Baudelaire wrote:

> Your eye rests upon a tree harmoniously bent by the wind;
> in a few seconds something which in a poet's brain would
> merely be a natural comparison becomes in yours a reality.
> First you give the tree your passions, your desire, or your
> melancholy; its groanings and oscillations become your own,
> and soon you are the tree.

Attempt the experience described by Charles
Baudelaire. Fix your eyes upon a tree, chair, wall . . . and
embody this tree, chair or wall. Now write.

Day 15

Imagination is the beginning of creation. You imagine what you desire, you will what you imagine and at last you create what you will.
—George Bernard Shaw

Day 16

Take a piece of tracing paper. Place it against this background. Write what you see. Now move the paper around to discover other legible "signs."

Discovery consists of seeing what everybody has seen
and thinking what nobody has thought.
—Albert Szent-Györgyi

Copy what you wrote yesterday (on
the tracing paper) onto several strips of
paper. Now assemble the strips and
paste them on a sheet of paper (or type
the text into your computer).

There can be no great poet without a spot of madness.
—Democritus

Many poems take the form of a list. Here, for example, is an excerpt of the poem "The Argument of His Book" by Robert Herrick:

I sing of brooks, of blossoms, birds, and bowers,
Of April, May, of June, and July-flowers;
I sing of May-poles, hock-carts, wassails, wakes,
Of bridegrooms, brides and of their bridal-cakes

Choose a subject that you can treat in the form of a list: your friends' names, the names of the streets in your town, brands of clothing, song titles or video games —anything will do. Read the list out loud. Try to develop a rhythm in the verses—either by rearranging the words or inserting some pauses.

Draw up an inventory of all the arranged (or scattered) objects you find in your desk drawer.

Here is what my trunk contains [. . .]
My big Mont Blanc sweater
A tie
Six dozen handkerchiefs
Three shirts
Six pajamas
Reams of white paper
Reams of white paper
And a lucky charm

—Blaise Cendrars

Day 19

A poet is a professional maker of verbal objects.
—W. H. Auden

Open your bathroom (or kitchen) door and make a list of everything you see. You can either randomly write down the names of the objects, or follow a particular order. For example, write what you see from the right side of the room to the left, or from the ceiling to the floor.

Day after day I loiter and explore
From door to door;
So many treasures lure
The curious mind. What histories obscure
They must immure!

—Bliss Carman,
from "Behind the Arras"

Do you know what you might find in a poet's coffin?
Saint-Pol Roux tells us:

A perfect harmony of distinct objects: cicadas, perfumes,
garlands, bees, nests, grapes, hearts, swords, fruits, thorns,
claws, talons, bleatings, chimeras, sphinxes, dice, mirrors,
goblets, rings, amphoras, trills, thyrsus, arpeggios, baubles,
peacocks, chimes, tiaras, rudders, trowels, beams, pouches,
iron, double-edge swords, chains, arrows, crosses, necklaces,
snakes, funerals, lightning, shields, buccina, trophies, urns,
clogs, breezes, waves, rainbows, laurels, palms, dew, smiles,
tears, rays, kisses, gold [. . .]

What would you find in the pockets of an absentminded
postman? In the backpack of a runaway child?
In the mind of a financial officer?
In . . .

Day 21

I know that poetry is indispensable, but to what I
could not say.
—Jean Cocteau

Search for and bookmark several
Internet sites devoted to poetry. You can
start with the following sites, which offer
many links:

www.poets.org
www.loc.gov/poetry
www.poetryarchive.org

The words that enlighten the soul are more precious than jewels.
—Hazrat Inayat Khan

When we pay close attention to the words we see and hear, we discover their connections to other things and the world. Look at some of the following words, below. Say them out loud.

Day 23

LOCOMOTIVE
BREATH
HORRIBLE
DROWSY
URCHIN
COMPUTER

Do not commit your poems to pages alone, sing them
I pray you.
—Virgil

Think of a word, listen to it, pro-
nounce it in every possible way, and
play with its sounds.

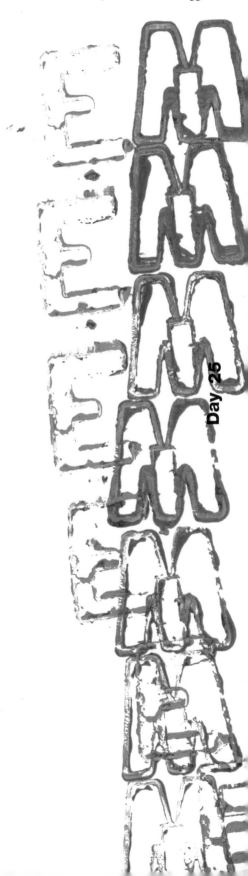

Here is the beginning of a playful poem:

> Oh! the potato
> the po ta to
> the po to ta
> the pa to to
> the to pa to

and the end of it:

> the ma to to
> the to ta mo
> the to ma ta
> the to ma to
> Ah! the tomato

—Raymond Federman,
"The Potato That Became a Tomato"

Try to fill in the missing lines. Now, using Federman's poem as a guide, trace the path between "caramel" and "carnival" or between "orange" and "garbage" or two other words of your choice.

Poetry is the rhythmical creation of beauty in words.
—Edgar Allan Poe

You have probably had to memorize some poems in your life. Copy some poems that you remember into your anthology—either in their entirety or in fragments.

Why should one read poetry?

Try to respond to this question. Then ask others around you and make a note of their answers.

I think that we read poems to create images in our head. (Anna)

I love poems because we can interpret them as we wish. (Luke)

I like reading poems because I like music, and poetry is music with words. (Justin)

I like poetry because it enables us to write about our woes. (Michael)

To be a poet is a condition, not a profession.
—Robert Frost

Poet, poet, poet . . .

Let's face it, the word "poet" (or "poetess!") doesn't sound so nice. What if you invented another name (or several): He (or she) who writes poetry is a . . .

Here is a poem about a poet:

This was a Poet—It is That
Distills amazing sense
From ordinary Meanings—
And Attar so immense

From the familiar species
That perished by the Door—
We wonder it was not Ourselves
Arrested it—before—

Of Pictures, the Discloser—
The Poet—it is He—
Entitles Us—by Contrast—
To ceaseless Poverty—

Of portion—so unconscious—
The Robbing—could not harm—
Himself—to Him—a Fortune—
Exterior—to Time—
          —Emily Dickinson,
     "This was a Poet—It is That"

Day 29

Now it's your turn . . . describe a poet.

What is a poem but a hazardous attempt at self-understanding?
—Robert Penn Warren

And you—why do you write poetry?

Poets long to be loved. But all that is necessary is that they should
be understood.
—Roy Fuller

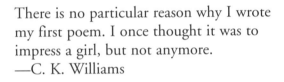
Do you remember the first poem you ever wrote? Describe it . . .

There is no particular reason why I wrote
my first poem. I once thought it was to
impress a girl, but not anymore.
—C. K. Williams

To be perfectly honest, I would have to
invent an answer, because I don't
remember my first poem. But already in
elementary school I was called Susie
Shakespeare, so I know that I started
poems at a very young age.
—Susie Morgenstern

I started writing in high school and then I met people who were writers and poets. We would talk
about poetry, read poetry . . . Five years after I
entered the United States, I published my first
poem.
—Charles Simic

I remember my first poem—it went into the
school magazine when I was about eight—and it
was the first really exciting thing that had ever
happened to me, this transition of my scribbled
words into printed form in that way.
—Elaine Feinstein

"Ugly Poem"

Make a list of words you find ugly, harsh, grating on the ears . . . Write a poem using as many of these words as you can. Don't forget: Your poem must be ugly!

Day 32

I never saw a purple cow,
I never hope to see one;
But I can tell you, anyhow,
I'd rather see than be one!
—Gelett Burgess

Today, try to find some humorous poems for your anthology. You can find some on this Internet site:

www.poetry-archive.com/collections/humorous_poems.html

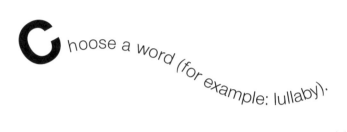

Choose a word (for example: lullaby).

Of what and of whom does this word make you think
(baby—sleep—song—cradle—mother—night . . .)?
Play with the letters of the word
(ex: lull—by—bull—buy—lay)
Now find words that rhyme with it
(ex: baby's cry—sigh—lie—pacify—butterfly)

Write a poem using as many of these assembled words as you can.

Day 34

Each word may not unfitly be compared to an invention.
—William Dwight Witney

The poem "Jabberwocky" by Lewis Carroll contains many new, invented words. Here are two verses from it.

'Twas brillig, and the slithy toves
Did gyre and gimble in the wabe:
All mimsy were the borogoves,
And the mome raths outgrabe.

"Beware the Jabberwock, my son!
The jaws that bite, the claws that catch!
Beware the Jubjub bird, and shun
The frumious Bandersnatch!"

Invent a definition for the following words, paying close attention to their meaning and sound:

Bric-a-brac
Cashmere
Ripple
Sizzling
Trinket
Ratchet

Gentle words, quiet words, are after all the most
powerful words. They are more convincing,
more compelling, more prevailing.
—Washington Gladden

Play with the following expressions
(and any others that come to mind):

The walls have ears
Cutting off your nose to spite your face
A wolf in sheep's clothing
Biting off more than one can chew

Day 36

Poetry is the purification of the language of the tribe.
—Stéphane Mallarmé

Day 37

Today's exercise involves the following rules:

1. Write a poem in which all 26 letters of the alphabet are used at least once (you can highlight them graphically).

2. Write a poem containing only 26 letters.

Choose one of these two rules . . . or invent another.

Poets are like children: when they're seated at their
desk, their feet don't touch the ground.
—Stanislaw Jerzy Lec

Do you remember the counting rhymes or poems you learned when you were a child? Copy some of them into your anthology.

Eeny, meeny, miny, moe
Catch a tiger by the toe
If he hollers let him go,
Eeny, meeny, miny, moe.

Day 38

What is a poet? A newborn at every age.
—Alain Bosquet

Write a counting rhyme.

Remember: A counting rhyme is a lyrical poem that is used to select a player who is "it" for games or other activities. The words are usually silly and play on sounds. They provide the beat for any gestures associated with the rhyme and help with memorization.

Some contemporary poets have played with this genre. Can you find some examples?

Here is the beginning and end of "Daffodils" by William Wordsworth; think of the lines as a starting point and an end point. It's up to you to connect the two.

I wandered lonely as a cloud

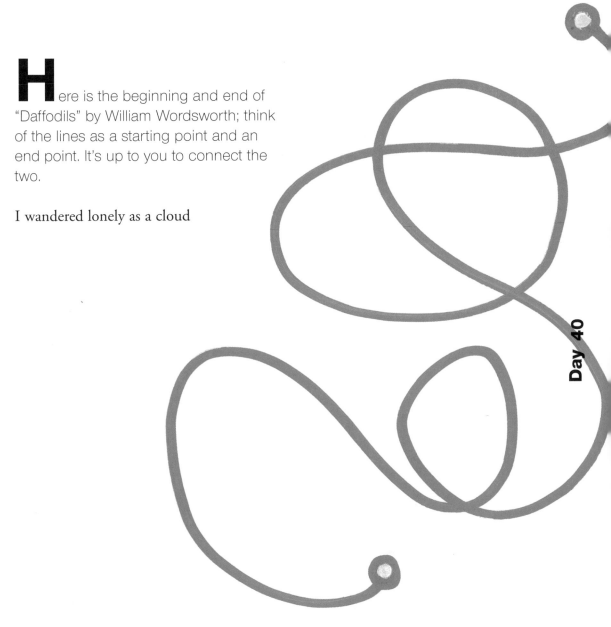

Day 40

And dances with the daffodils.

Writing is an exploration. You start from nothing and
learn as you go.
—E. L. Doctorow

Here are the first two lines of
"When the Year Grows Old" by Edna St.
Vincent Millay. Think of it as the start of
a path. Now follow it.

I cannot but remember
When the year grows old

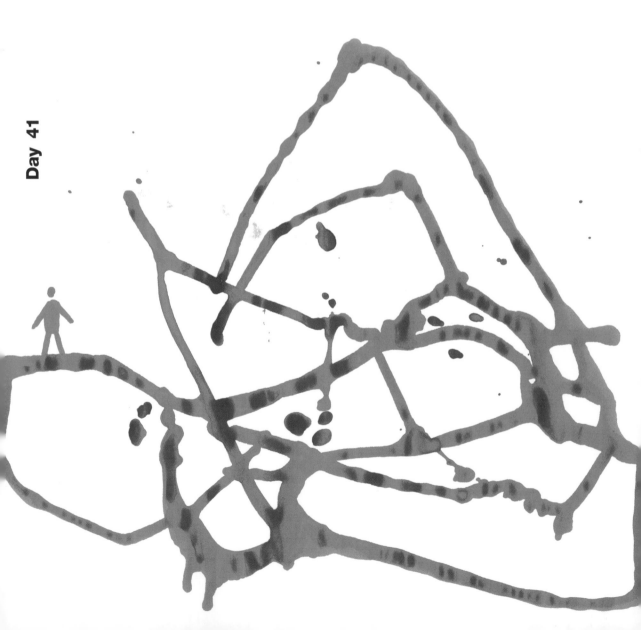

Poetry is like mining radium. To gain
a gram you must labor a year.
—Vladimir Mayakovsky

Copy the beginning of several
poems into your anthology: the first
verse, first sentence, or first stanza.

A short saying often contains much wisdom.
—Sophocles

Find some short poems and copy them into your anthology. Here are some examples:

There was presented to me a papaya,
And I returned for it a beautiful Ju-gem;
Not as a return for it,
But that our friendship might be lasting.

—From *Shi Jing* (The Book of Odes)
Translation by James Legge

Let thy speech be short,
comprehending much in a few words.
—Ecclesiasticus

Here are some monostiches—poems in a single line. One of the most famous is by Guillaume Apollinaire:

SINGER
And the sole string of the sea trumpets

Some other examples:

From your mouth, o woman,
flows a milk of song
—Georges Friendenkraft

Sailboat carrying off the sun in its yards
—Emmanuel Lochac

Day 44

Now it's your turn . . .

Poetry is what's lacking.
—Éric Sarner

Aunit of verse consisting of two lines is called a distich.

The apparition of these faces in the crowd;
Petals on a wet, black bough.

                              —Ezra Pound

Heaven from all creatures hides the book of Fate,
All but the page prescrib'd, their present state.
                              —Alexander Pope,
                    from "An Essay on Man"

Now you write one . . .

People today don't want a poet. They keep asking me
for a radio . . .
—Naguib Mafouz

Write a short poem and record it on your answering machine as a greeting.

A poem is an intimate refuge—a land of peace.
—Zoé Valdès

An exercise in brevity: Write a short poem having only three, four, or five lines. Be daring, playful, spontaneous . . .

Her tears are spent, but no dreams come.
She can hear the others singing through the night.
She has lost his love. Alone with her beauty,
She leans till dawn on her incense pillow.
—Chu-i Po, "A Song of the Palace"

Day 47

Day 48

Aone-minute poem:
Take out your watch, paper, and pen,
and write a poem in under a minute, no
more. And, since you have a good five
minutes to spare,

write five of them.

Poetry is life distilled.
—Gwendolyn Brooks

A poem in a day

Write down the words that pop into your head the moment you wake up. Continue to do so at regular intervals during the course of the day and allow your text to incorporate the situations and places you find yourself in . . . Specify, or not, the time and place where you wrote.

Day 49

To me, every hour of the light and dark is a miracle,
Every cubic inch of space is a miracle.
                                    —Walt Whitman, "Miracles"

Today you will explore vocabulary: Take out your forgotten
trunk of rare words, dust it off, polish it, and attempt to compose a text that exceeds your wildest ambitions. Why not?
Your efforts could culminate in something like this:

Basse-Pointe, Diamant, Tartant and Caravelle
shekels of gold, flotation planes attacked by sheaves and corncockles [. . .]
smoky armadillos
O the krumen jokesters of my surf!
                                        —Aime Cesaire

Comb through your dictionary for some hidden gems. Use
what you find to write a unique poem.

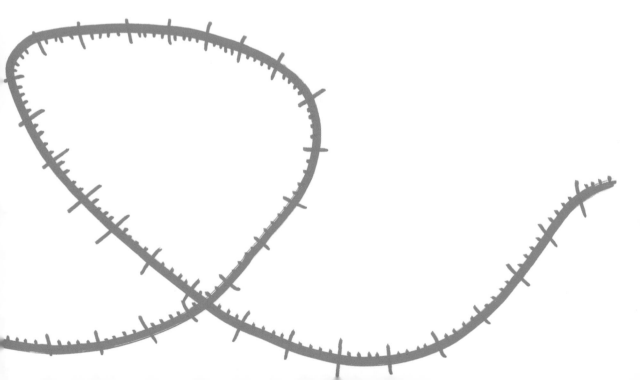

Language is never too poor for the poet.
—Novalis

A modest poem:

Write a text using only the fifty most common words of the English language. Here they are:

The, of, and, a, to, in, is, you, that, it, he, for, was, on, are, as, with, his, they, at, be, this, from, I, have, or, by, one, had, not, but, what, all, were, when, we, there, can, an, your, which, their, said, if, do, will, each, about, how, up

Poetry—all of it!—is a voyage into the unknown.
—Vladimir Mayakovsky

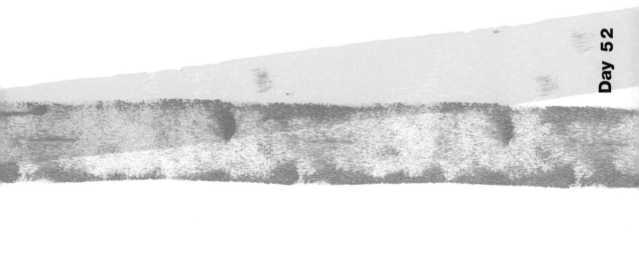

Search for poems written in a foreign language that you are familiar with, or for translated poems from a country that you love and dream of.

Day 52

One who speaks a foreign language just a little takes
more pleasure in it than one who speaks it well.
Enjoyment belongs to those who know things halfway.
—Friedrich Nietzsche

A polyglot poem

Write a poem made up of words from
several different languages. Here are
some

words
mots
Wörter
lacuna
woorden
to start . . .

Smithereens recuperate parallax
And Bloemen aujourd'hui couteau.
Frangere bellus . . .
Faulenzen! Laggen!
Frémissement . . .

l'hiver risere?
Paradox!
Brauchen Vloerkleed nyctalope
Sonne?
Arbor!
Mensa Segel . . . Gordijnen.
Klein ontology!

In poetry . . . the order of the words
is the order of your heart.
—Peter A. Rosado

Select a poem for a loved one and read it to him or her over the telephone.

Day 54

Poetry is the gap that separates words
from their meanings.
—Jean-Michel Maulpoix

Here is part of a verse written by Charles Baudelaire:

We shall have beds full of light perfumes

Replace the word "beds" with another one-syllable word. Then continue to replace every other word with another one having the same number of syllables. How far can you go?

This exercise follows the same principle as yesterday,
except this time, start with an excerpt of a poem in prose;
you can change one, two, or even three words each time.

In a lovely garden, where the rays of an autumn sun seemed
to linger pleasantly, under a green-tinged sky in which golden
clouds seemed to float like traveling continents, four beautiful
children, four boys, probably tired of playing, were chatting
amongst themselves.

—Charles Baudelaire,
from "Vocations"

Read each new version of your text out loud.
Listen to how it changes, how it evolves . . .

Day 56

A poem is never finished, only abandoned.
—Paul Valéry

Today, try some new writing positions:

lying on your back,
sitting cross-legged,
standing on one foot . . .

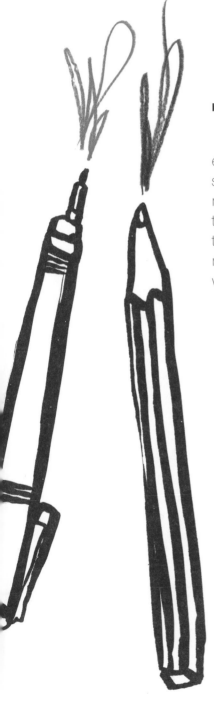

In art, the hand can never execute anything higher
than the heart can imagine.
—Ralph Waldo Emerson

Take a large sheet of paper and either a pencil or a felt-tip pen. Start scribbling. Pay attention on the movements of your hand and then, little by little, start writing some words. Go back to scribbling, but this time vary your movements, and by extension, your words.

Day 58

Finally, assemble and organize everything you've written.

Poetry remembers that it was an oral art before it was a
written art.
—Jorge Luis Borges

Today, memorize a poem by
a contemporary author. Start by
reciting it several times out loud;
vary the intensity, flow, and the
pauses you leave between the
words . . .

Take up the activity of Day 13, but
with the following modification:
Write a one-line poem

Write a two-line poem by adding a line to
the previous poem

Write a three-line poem by adding a line
to the second poem
and so on . . .

Advice: Forget about rhyming. Instead,
play with the breaks and especially the
differences between the lengths of the
verses.

Day 60

Poetry should . . . strike the reader as a wording
of his own highest thoughts, and appear almost
a remembrance.
—John Keats

Day 61

Choose a poem
(not a very long one) from your anthology.
Copy it, but this time erase some of the
words (between three and six).
You will end up with an entirely new
poem. Copy a third poem, and erase
some of the words again. And so on.

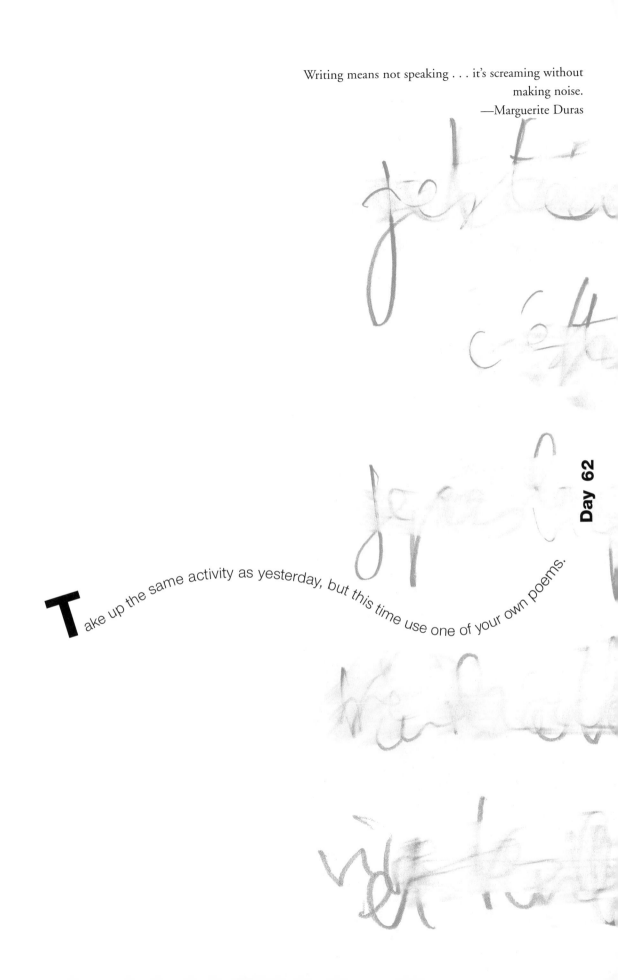

Writing means not speaking . . . it's screaming without making noise.
—Marguerite Duras

Day 62

Take up the same activity as yesterday, but this time use one of your own poems.

We are all drafts of a text that will never be corrected.
—Roberto Juarroz

Write about yourself writing: Where are you, what time is it, what noises do you hear, what is the lighting like, what is your attitude, what gestures do you make, what tools are you using . . . ?

What do you feel when you write a poem? Describe (or at least try to) the process of writing: your movements, emotions, sensations, conscious or unconscious thoughts . . .

When I write a poem, I see an image behind each word, and behind that image, another word.

—Clo Duri Bezzola

When I write a poem, I always write it in one breath, in a flash . . . I have never written a poem by following a conscious methodology . . . I write poetry as if spitting out a lump of something, and I feel catharsis by doing so.

—Masayo Koike

When I write a poem, it's like taking a huge block of stone or marble and I keep chipping away at it, chipping away until I finally get to the nugget that's in the middle.

—Eileen Kernaghan

Day 64

. . . and what if a poem directed man's path . . .
—Gaston Miron

Choose a poem for three different people you like (a different poem for each). Send it to them by e-mail or regular mail.

Here are the titles of several poems. Choose one and write a poem based on its title.

THE LOCKLESS DOOR

THERE'S A CERTAIN SLANT OF LIGHT

PARTING AT DAWN

Day 66

WHAT ARE YEARS?

WHEN I THINK ABOUT MYSELF

Poetry is heard with the ears but seen only with the mind.
—Octavio Paz

Listen to some recordings of poems on the Internet. You will find some on the following site:

http://www.loc.gov/poetry/archive.html

Day 67

A mobile poem

We're going out today! Stroll through the streets or paths of your town. Listen to the rhythm of your footsteps and slowly match words to them. Visualize the words in your head, whisper them, or scream them, it's up to you. Once you get home, write them down.

Day 68

A poet knows how to play a harp without chords, and he has an answer to those who claim not to have heard its music.

—Lao Tzu

Read this text aloud, placing emphasis on the repeated words.

Half a league, half a league,
Half a league onward,
All in the valley of Death
Rode the six hundred:
"Forward, the Light Brigade!
Charge for the guns" he said:
Into the valley of Death
Rode the six hundred.

  —Alfred, Lord Tennyson,
from "The Charge of the Light Brigade"

Find some other poems in which the use of repetition creates the rhythm. Copy them into your anthology.

Poetry: writing that formulates a concentrated imaginative awareness of experience in language chosen and arranged to create a specific emotional response through meaning, sound, and rhythm.
—Merriam-Webster Dictionary

Read the following poem by Edgar Allan Poe, "The Bells," which has been slightly changed:

HEAR the sledges with the bells,
　　Silver bells!
What a world of merriment their melody foretells!
　How they tinkle,
　　In the icy air of night!
　While the stars, that oversprinkle
　All the heavens, seem to twinkle
　　With a crystalline delight;
　　Keeping time,
　　In a sort of Runic rhyme,
To the tintinnabulation that so musically wells
　From the bells,
　　Bells,—
　From the jingling and the tinkling of the bells.

In the original text, some of the words were repeated. Can you restore the repe-titions in order to reveal the original rhythm of the poem? Try it several times.

Rhythm, more rhythm, always rhythm.
—Henri Meschonnic

Read this poem fragment out loud:

A Bird came down the Walk—
He did not know I saw—
He bit an Angleworm in halves
And ate the fellow, raw,

And then he drank a Dew
From a convenient Grass—
And then hoped sidewise to the Wall
To let a Beetle pass.

> —Emily Dickinson,
> from "A Bird Came Down the Walk"

Count the number of syllables in each verse. Does the line contain six syllables, seven, or more? Does each verse have an odd or even number of syllables?

Reread some of your poems and see if you can find a pattern to the number of syllables in each verse.

The poet makes himself a seer by a long, prodigious,
and rational disordering of all the senses.
—Arthur Rimbaud

Write a poem (either in verse or
prose), alternating the number of syllables
in each line.

A Sonnet is a moment's monument.
—Dante Gabriel Rossetti

The sonnet isn't dead (nor, for that matter, are the alexandrine and other traditional forms of poetry). But today's poets take some liberties with the form. Note, for example, the absence of ten-syllable lines, the standard for sonnets, in this excerpt from "Sonnet 6" by Rainer Maria Rilke:

They more adeptly bend the willow's branches
who have experience of the willow's roots.

And the grammatical breaks in this excerpt from "Sonnet 12: After Robert Duncan" by Wanda Coleman:

my earliest dreams linger/wronged spirits
who will not rest/dusky crows astride

TWELVE +

The alexandrine (a line of twelve syllables) is not a maximum; one can easily write a poem with longer lines, such as this stanza from "The Raven" by Edgar Allen Poe:

Once upon a midnight dreary, while I pondered, weak and weary
Over many a quaint and curious volume of forgotten lore,
While I nodded, nearly napping, suddenly there came a tapping
As of some one gently rapping, rapping at my chamber door.

Invent your own form (13, 14, 17, or 20 lines); use it to write a poem.

Day 74

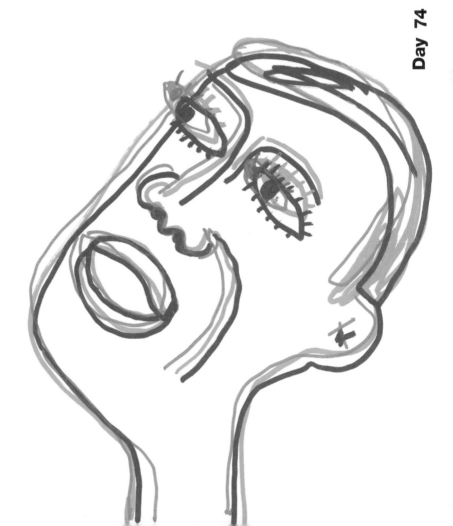

Anything is fit material for poetry.
—William Carlos Williams

Here are a few scattered fragments
from a poem by Robert Lowell ("Children of
Light"). Fill in the rest . . .

Our fathers

gardens

of light

houses built

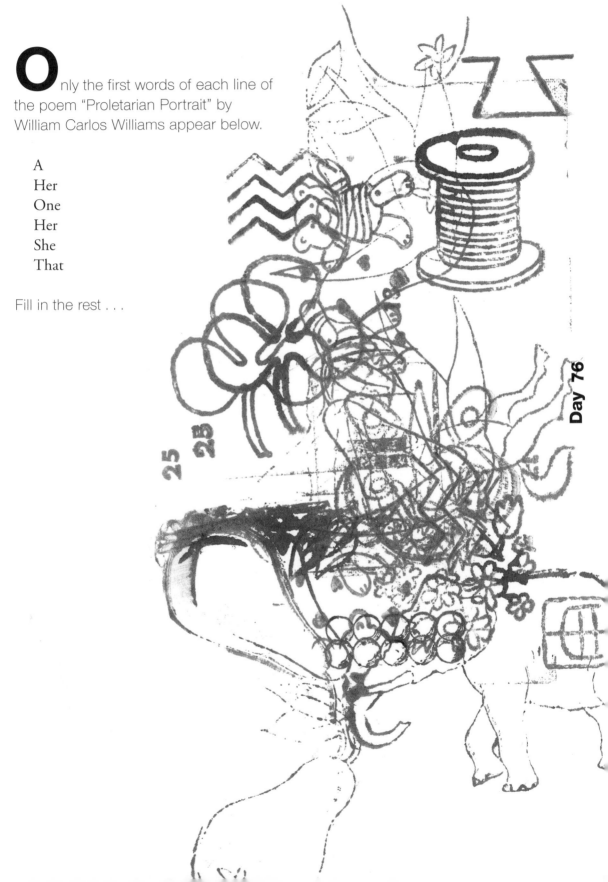

To know is nothing at all; to imagine is everything.
—Anatole France

Only the first words of each line of the poem "Proletarian Portrait" by William Carlos Williams appear below.

A
Her
One
Her
She
That

Fill in the rest . . .

Day 76

To name an object is to deprive a poem of three-fourths of its pleasure, which consists in a little-by-little guessing game; the ideal is to suggest.
—Wallace Stevens

Below are two lines taken from the middle of a poem by W. H. Davies ("The Rain").

And when the Sun comes out,
After this Rain shall stop

Write what comes before and after them.

One should give this title to every poem:
"How to live joyfully."
—Francis Ponge

And so today, do just that. Give today's poem this title: How to live joyfully

Day 78

O the joy of my spirit—it is uncaged—it darts like lightning!
—Walt Whitman

A poet must be a teacher of hope.
—Jean Giono

John Keats, one of England's greatest poets, once said that "poetry should be great and unobtrusive, a thing which enters one's soul . . ." Here is an excerpt from his poem "To Hope":

When by my solitary hearth I sit,
When no fair dreams before my "mind's eye" flit,
And the bare heath of life presents no bloom;
Sweet Hope, ethereal balm upon me shed,
And wave thy silver pinions o'er my head.

Now write your own poem entitled "To Hope."

Start with a letter—whichever one you choose.

Now find some words that start with it.

> [. . .]
> *m*
> as in multitudes
> mornings and myths
> *m* for masticate
> memory mantles
> —Lionel Ray

Continue . . .

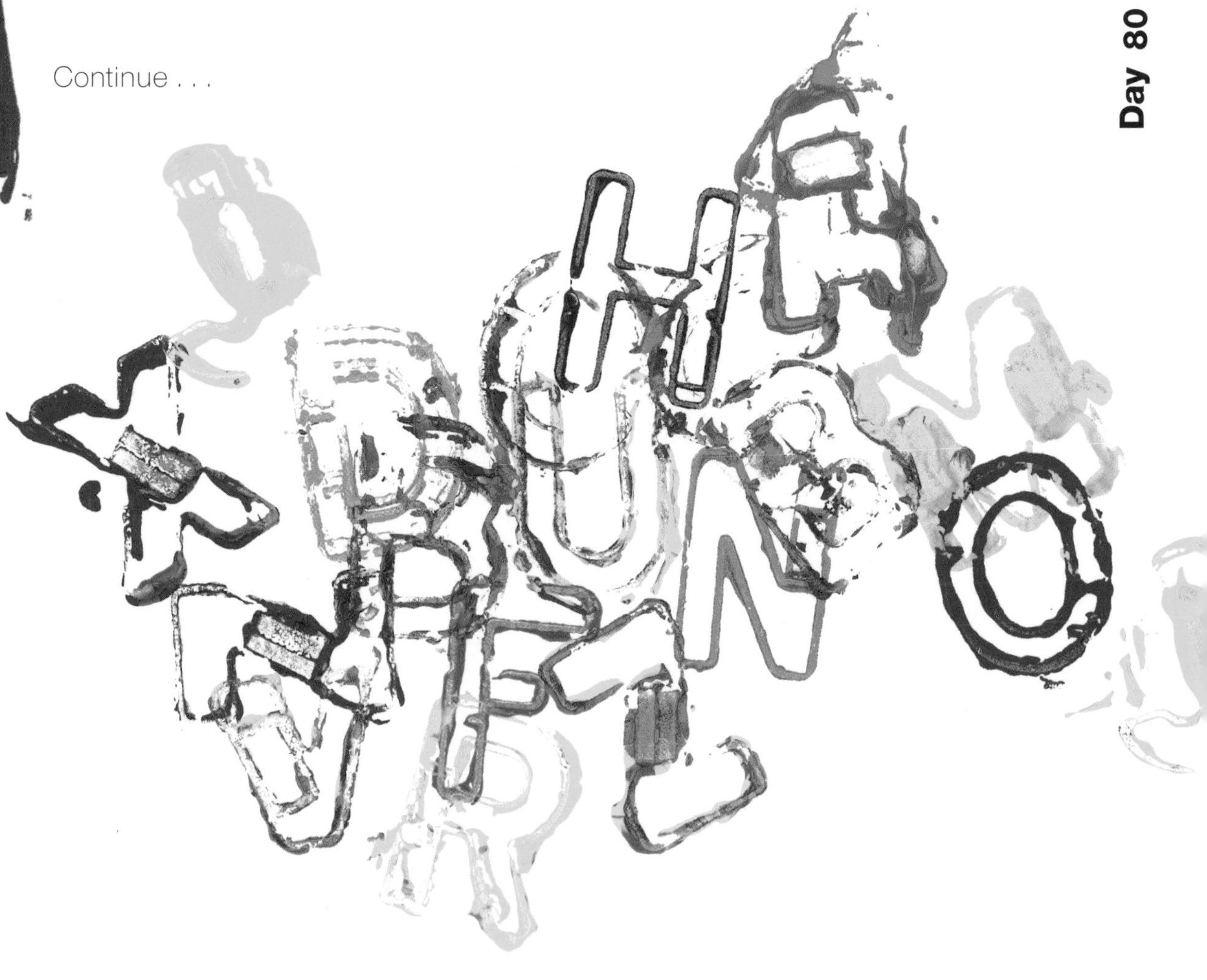

Day 80

A poet doesn't write; he listens.
—Jean-Marie Barnaud

His death, which happen'd in his berth,
At forty-odd befell:
They went and told the sexton, and
The sexton toll'd the bell.
                    —Thomas Hood,
            from "Faithless Sally Brown"

In the style of Thomas Hood, play with the homonyms of words. Here are some examples:

Idle idol idyl
Wood would
Cents sense scents
Or ore oar
Peek peak pique
etc . . .

There are some poets who don't mince their words—
they chew them.
—Jean L'Anselme

A poem to chew on

Construct your own poem based on
the repetition of a sound, syllable, or word

It is well known that words are not used solely to render meaning. They play, they make love. They compose music.
—Maryse Condé

[Ai'ryte]

means: I write
I rite
Eye right
Ay write

Can you think up other ways to write the following words:

Word
Poetry
Poem
Literature

Compose a text including all the variants of your chosen word.

Every word carries its own surprises and offers
its own rewards to the reflective mind.
—George A. Miller

What if the word "love" was written "luv"; would
it mean the same thing? Change the spelling of the
following words (invent several spellings for each
word):

Rhythm
Poetry
Grammar
Elephant
Galaxy

Day 84

When words change their appearance, do we interpret them differently?

A poet must leave traces of his passage, not proof.
—René Char

Look at the titles of some poems, either by leafing through a poetry anthology or searching on the Internet. Make a note of the ones that intrigue, disturb, or inspire you.

Today, you have an "inoremass" (ha!) task: to invent new words, like Lewis Carroll does in "Jabberwocky":

'Twas brillig and the slithy toves
Did gyre and gimble in the wabe.
All mimsy were the borogroves
And the mome raths outgrabe . . .

Imagine the guests at a fantastic party, an intergalactic meeting of envoys from every planet of the universe . . .

Day 86

Poetry isn't literature.
—Jacques Roubaud

Find some titles of poetry **collections** that pique your curiosity, either at the library or on the Internet.

For example:

The Fact of a Doorframe, Adrienne Rich
Meditations in an Emergency, Frank O'Hara
Dismantling the Silence, Charles Simic
Montage of a Dream Deferred, Langston Hughes
Braving the Elements, James Merrill

Now invent some of your own . . .

After all, commonplaces are the great poetic truths.
—Robert Louis Stevenson

Open your kitchen cabinets or refrigerator doors. Scan the brand names of the food items you see and use them to write a consumerist poem.

Poetry should continually remain in contact with the
speech and the life around it . . .
—Louise Bogan

Urban poetry

While strolling around town, make a
note of the signs, stores, and trade
names that you see. Incorporate them
into a poem.

All afternoon the shadows have been building
A city of their own within the streets [. . .]
—Charles Tomlinson,
from "All Afternoon"

The theory behind a list: jumble together small pieces
that have nothing to do with each other.
—Pierre Menard

Cut some sentences, words, or
images out of a newspaper or magazine.
Put them all together and leave the rest
to your imagination.

Take a newspaper.
Take a pair of scissors.
Choose from the paper an article as long as you plan to make your poem.
Cut out the article.
Then carefully cut out each of the words that make up this article and put them in a bag.
Shake it gently.

—Tristan Tzara,
from "To Make a Dadaist Poem"

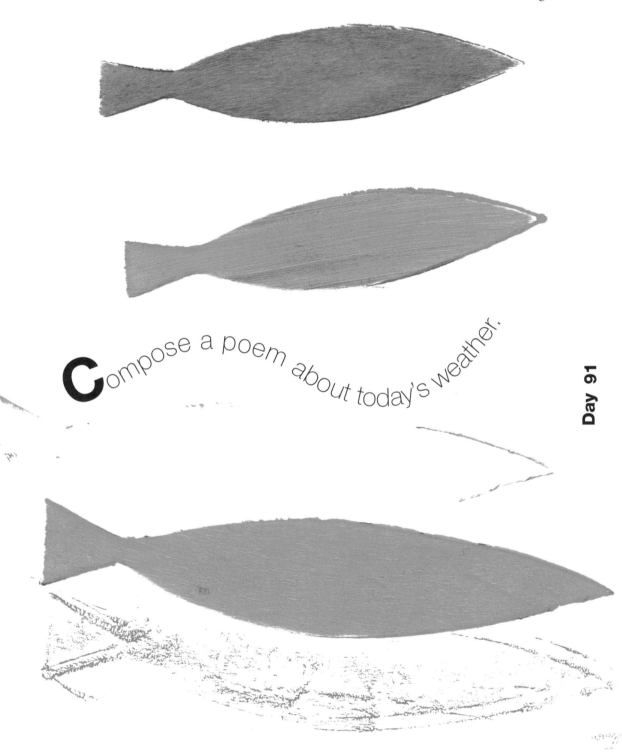

Compose a poem about today's weather.

Day 91

The poet gives us his essence, but prose takes the mold
of the body and mind.
—Virginia Wolf

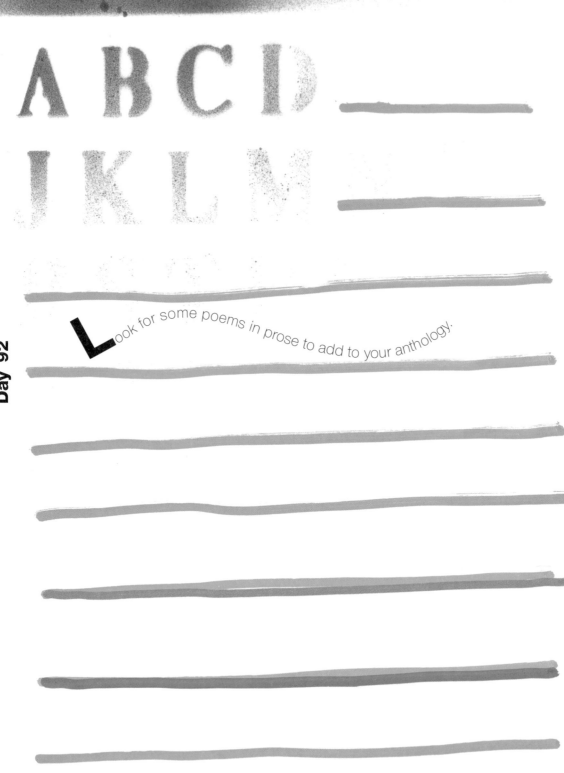

Look for some poems in prose to add to your anthology.

Here is the beginning of "Hands"
from *Winesburg, Ohio,* a novel by
Sherwood Anderson:

> Upon the half decayed veranda of a small frame house that
> stood near the edge of a ravine near the town of Winesburg,
> Ohio, a fat little old man walked nervously up and down.

Starting from this first line (or modifying it
if you prefer), continue the prose . . .

Day 93

Eloquence is the poetry of prose.
—William C. Bryant

Write a poem in prose on the theme of "looking" by applying the following rule: Each sentence must start with **the same word.** Choose from the following list:

you
see
on
where
window
line

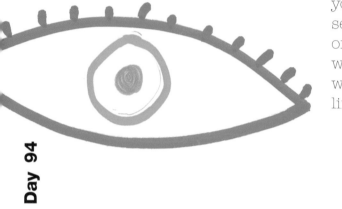

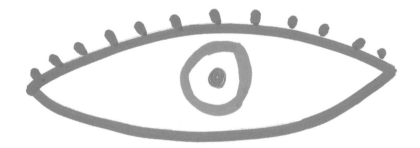
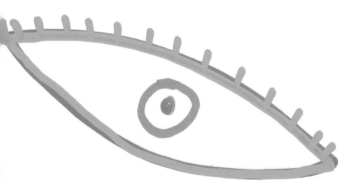

Poetry is prose at lift-off.
—Leon-Paul Fargue

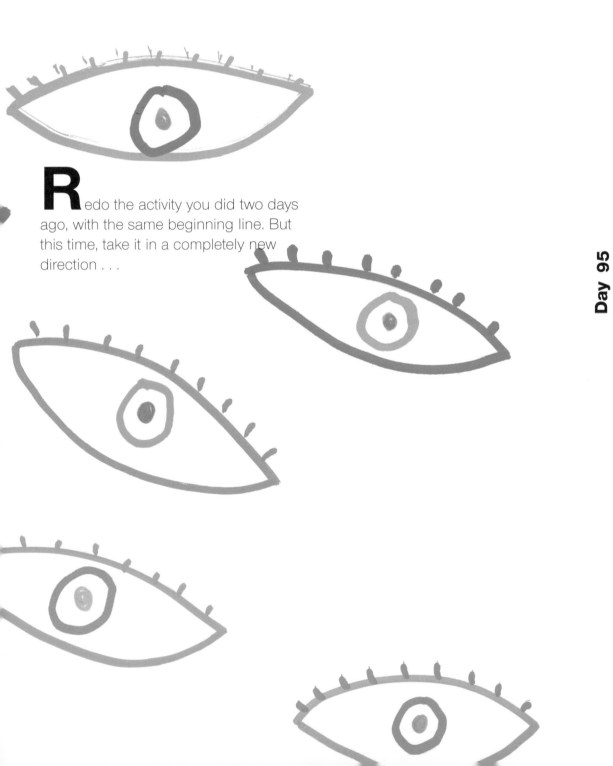

Redo the activity you did two days ago, with the same beginning line. But this time, take it in a completely new direction . . .

Day 95

Poems celebrate the pure solidity
of my illusion of the world.
—Ted Hughes

Take one of your poems in prose
and cut it into free verse. Read both
versions aloud.

Compare them.

Read this text by William Barnes out loud:

> Aye, at that time our days wer but vew,
> An our lim's wer but small, an a-growen;
> An then the feair worold wer new,
> An' life wer all hopevul an' gay;
> An' the times o' the sprouten o' leaves,
> An the cheak-burnen seasons o' mowen,
> An' binden o' red-headed sheaves,
> Wer all wecome seasons o' jay [. . .]

Now take one of your own texts and invent a new spelling for it.

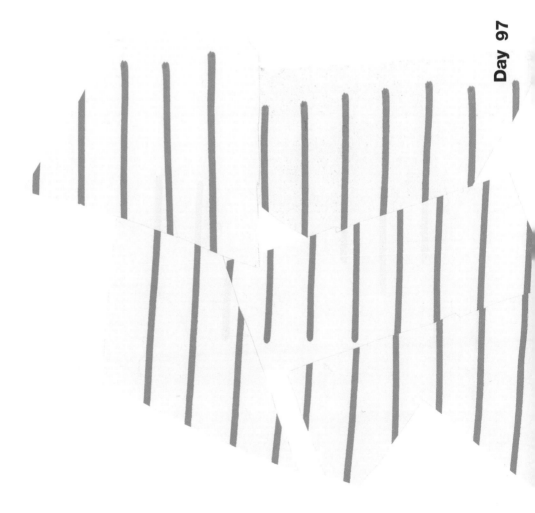

Not philosophy, after all, not humanity, just the sheer
joyous power of song, is the primal thing in poetry.
—Max Beerbohm

Find some examples of poems that were set to music and copy them in your anthology. Read the poems out loud and listen for their musicality. Here is an exerpt from one such poem by Robert Burns, "Auld Lang Syne." Do you find that you are starting to sing the words?

Should auld acquaintance be forgot,
    And never brought to mind?
Should auld acquaintance be forgot,
    And auld lang syne!

Chorus: For auld lang syne, my dear,
    For auld lang syne.
We'll tak a cup o' kindness yet,
    For auld lang syne.

Here is a poem by Emily Dickinson:

The Brain—is wider than the Sky—
For—put them side by side—
The one the other will contain
With ease—and You—beside—
　　　　　　—Emily Dickinson,
　　from "The Brain is wider than the Sky"

Rewrite this poem several times, playing
with the insertion of capitalization and
punctuation, either liberally or in abun-
dance. You'll probably end up with several
different versions of the poem . . .

Day 99

Day 100

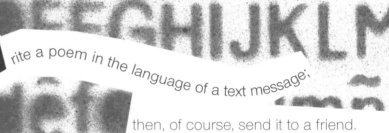

W rite a poem in the language of a text message;

then, of course, send it to a friend.

One writes because one has a burning desire to objectify
what is indispensable to one's happiness to express.
—Marianne Moore

Definition: A simile is a comparison between two things that aren't normally related to each other. The comparison is typically made explicit by using "like" or "as." Here are some examples:

Like a skein of loose silk blown against a wall
She walks by the railing of a path in
Kensington Gardens
                    —Ezra Pound,
                        from "The Garden"

My love is like a red, red rose
   That's newly sprung in June:
My love is like the melody
   That's sweetly played in tune.
                    —Robert Burns,
                        from "A Red, Red Rose"

Sorrow like a ceaseless rain
beats upon my heart
                    —Edna St. Vincent Millay,
                        from "Sorrow"

Shall I compare thee to a summer's day?
Thou art more lovely and more temperate.
                    —William Shakespeare,
                        from "Sonnet 18"

Find some other examples of similes from poetry and copy them into your anthology.

Day 101

Imagery is two words coming together to create a new world.
—Saint-Pol Roux

Below are two lists of words. Create similes by comparing a word in list A with a word in list B.

A	B
house	boat
pants	dance
grandmother	forgiveness
letter	line
roof	pebble
telephone	finger
raindrop	rest
arithmetic	chair
windshield	keyboard
shame	railroad
light	turkey
abyss	breath
stomach	tree

Here's an example, by Elizabeth Bishop:

> his brown skin hung in strips
> like ancient wallpaper.
> —Elizabeth Bishop,
> from "The Fish"

Pick one of your similes from
yesterday and use it to begin writing
a new poem.

Everything you can imagine is real.
—Pablo Picasso

W

hat is being described in the following poem excerpts?

1. How countlessly they congregate
O'er our tumultuous snow,
                    —Robert Frost

2. . . . a pair of ragged claws
Scuttling across the floors of silent seas.
                    —T. S. Eliot

3. Who lips the roots o' the shore, and glides
Superb on unreturning tides.
                    —Rupert Brooke

4. He clasps the crag with crooked hands;
Close to the sun in lonely lands,
Ring'd with the azure world, he stands.

The wrinkled sea beneath him crawls;
He watches from his mountain walls,
And like a thunderbolt he falls.
                    —Alfred, Lord Tennyson

Answers:
1. stars; from "Stars"
2. a crab; from "The Love Song of
J. Alfred Prufrock"
3. a fish; from "The Fish"
4. an eagle; from "The Eagle"

Poetry should be great and unobtrusive, a thing which enters
into one's soul, and does not startle it or amaze it with itself, but
with its subject.
—John Keats

Pure of heart and therefore hungry,
All night long you have sung in vain—
Oh, this final broken indrawn breath
Among the green indifferent trees!
Yes, I have gone like a piece of driftwood,
I have let my garden fill with weeds . . .
I bless you for your true advice
To live as pure a life as yours.
—Li Shang-yin,
"A Cicada"

Now it's your turn:

What amazes you?

The greatest thing by far is to be a master of metaphor.
—Aristotle

Definition: A metaphor is a figure of speech that establishes a direct relationship between two seemingly dissimilar subjects. In this excerpt from a poem by Percy Bysshe Shelley—"A poet is a nightingale, who sits in darkness and sings to cheer its own solitude with sweet sounds"—the singing nightingale is a metaphor for writing poetry.

Here are some other examples:

All the world's a stage,
And all the men and women merely players;
They have their exits and their entrances
—William Shakespeare,
from *As You Like It*

The yellow fog that rubs its back upon the window-panes
—T. S. Eliot,
from "The Love Song of J. Alfred Prufrock"

Shoes, secret face of my inner life:
Two gaping toothless mouths
—Charles Simic,
from "My Shoes"

Which of these metaphors allows you "see" the most? Search for other metaphors in your poems.

> The metaphor is an origin, the origin of an image that acts directly, immediately.
> —Gaston Bachelard

Create metaphors by directly relating a word from list A to a word in list B. You can do it in two stages: Create a comparison first and then erase the word used to compare the two things.

A	B
night	creak
iceberg	braid
sky	honey
bowl	feet
wild	laugh
fog	palm
source	poem
knot	murmur
concrete	parking
software	whiteness
thigh	shell
clock	pleasure
harmony	case

Example:
1. The fog is like a cat. A cat has feet.
2. **The fog comes**
   on little cat feet.

—Carl Sandburg,
from "The Fog"

Imagination could hardly do without metaphor . . .
—Robert A. Nisbet

Pick one of your metaphors from yesterday and use it to begin writing a new poem.

"What does that mean?" is the reproach we make to
poets when they fail to move us.
—Max Jacob

Sometimes, when you're reading a
poem, you might ask yourself "But
what does it mean?" You might even
have cried, "It has no meaning!" Copy
at least one of these poems in your
anthology.

The poem is an original and unique creation, but it is also reading and recitation: participation.
—Octavio Paz

The poet Edward Hirsch has said the following about reading poetry:

Read poems to yourself in the middle of the night. Turn on a single lamp and read them while you're alone in an otherwise dark room . . . read them when you're wide awake in the early morning, fully alert. Say them over to yourself in a place where silence reigns and the din of the culture—the constant buzzing noise that surrounds us—has momentarily stopped. These poems have come from a great distance to find you . . .

Pick one of the poems that you deemed "incomprehensible" yesterday and be patient with it. Take your time and concentrate on every line. Read and reread it, as often as you can. Wait for the poem to take shape in your mind . . .

Once more: Read the "incomprehensible" poem from yesterday. Aloud.
In one breath, and then in fragments.

How did it go this time?

Poetry allows us to see with our ears.
—Jean-Pierre Depetris

A step-by-step poem . . .

Write a poem using only one-syllable words,
such as in this excerpt:

Here a star, and there a star
Some lose their way.

—Emily Dickinson,
from "Life"

Create a rhythm by tapping against
a table, beating a drum, or clapping
your hands. When you've found one,
write a poem to it.

Day 113

Poetry cannot be found in life or things. It is only what
we make of it—what we add.
—Pierre Reverdy

Long/short
(or short/long)

In this exercise, the first line can be as long as
you like, but the second can only have one or
two words (or vice versa).

> i have found what you are like
> the rain
>
> —e. e. cummings,
> from "i have found what you are like"

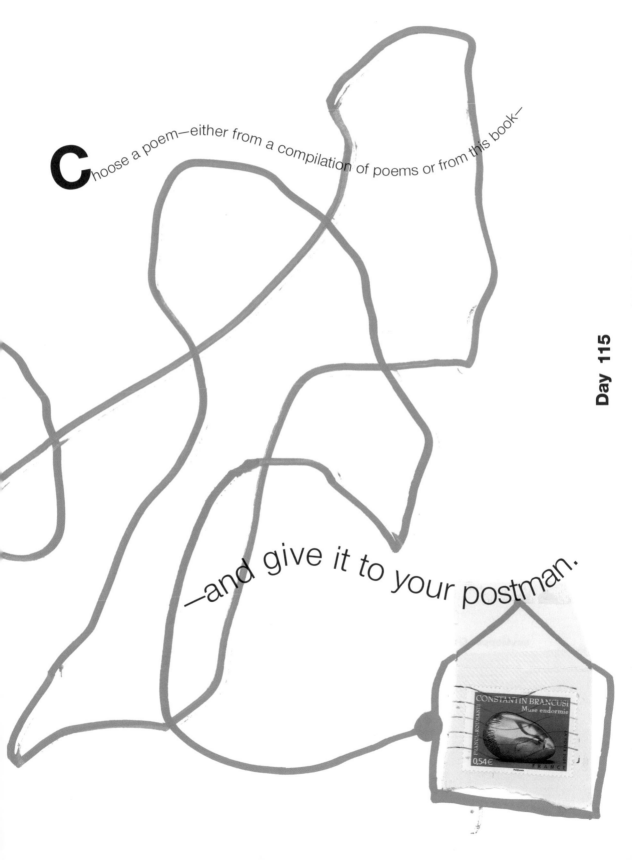

Every poem can be considered in two ways—as what
the poet has to say, and as a thing which he makes.
—C. S. Lewis

Choose a poem—either from a compilation of poems or from this book—

Day 115

—and give it to your postman.

A poem is an ear—not a mouth.
—Serge Pey

Noise poem

Close your eyes. Listen. Pay attention to the sounds you hear. Find the words that correspond to them (as though your poem was a musical score). You can also draw the images you associate with the sounds.

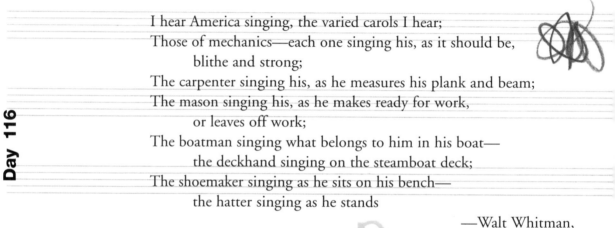

I hear America singing, the varied carols I hear;
Those of mechanics—each one singing his, as it should be,
    blithe and strong;
The carpenter singing his, as he measures his plank and beam;
The mason singing his, as he makes ready for work,
    or leaves off work;
The boatman singing what belongs to him in his boat—
    the deckhand singing on the steamboat deck;
The shoemaker singing as he sits on his bench—
    the hatter singing as he stands

—Walt Whitman,
from "Song of Myself"

Day 116

All music is what awakes from you
When you are reminded by the instruments.
—Walt Whitman

Poetry of sounds

Write a poem using interjections,
musical terms, or sound effects.

This is the song that the famous philospher
Haeckel was humming while strolling in his garden
on July 3, 1911 (according to a witness).

Wimmbamm Bumm
Wimm Bammbumm
Wimm Bamm Bumm

Wimm Bammbumm
Wimm Bamm Bumm
Wimmbamm Bumm

Wimm Bamm Bumm
Wimmbamm Bumm
Wimm Bammbumm.

—Joachim Ringelnatz

Prose talks and poetry sings.
—Franz Grillparzer

Imitation poetry

Write a poem that imitates various sounds.

Whirl ye the deadly voo-doo rattle,
Harry the uplands,
Steal all the cattle,
Rattle-rattle, rattle-rattle,
Bing.
Boomlay, boomlay, boomlay, BOOM

—Vachel Lindsay,
from "The Congo"

Read this poem by Gerard Manley Hopkins out loud:

Repeat that, repeat,
Cuckoo, bird, and open ear wells, heart-
    springs, delightfully sweet,
With a ballad, with a ballad, a rebound
Off trundled timber and scoops of the hillside
    ground, hollow hollow hollow ground:
The whole landscape flushes on a sudden at
    the sound.

—Gerard Manley Hopkins,
"Repeat That, Repeat"

Day 119

Do you hear how the usage of repetition and rhyme lends a sense of rhythm to the poem?

Poetry, for me, is the opposite of an exercise in style—
it's an adventure in language.
—Sappho

Write a poem composed only of
interjections (Ah! Oh! Huh?)
and onomatopoeia (Bang! Buzz!
Clink! Slurp!)

<blockquote>
Different times and different spaces are combined in a
here and now that is everywhere at once.
—Octavio Paz
</blockquote>

Below you'll find a compressed
text: All the punctuation and line
breaks have been removed. It's up
to you to cut the text in various lines,
restoring the poem's original spacing
and rhythm.

two roads diverged in a yellow wood and sorry I could not travel both and be
one traveler long I stood and looked down one as far as I could to where it
bent in the undergrowth then took the other as just as fair and having perhaps
the better claim because it was grassy and wanted wear though as for that the
passing there had worn them really about the same

—Robert Frost,
from "The Road Not Taken"

Day 121

Silence is so accurate.
—Mark Rothko

 an you "read" the white spaces in a poem? For example, in:

A rounded face
In the dark corner of the sky

The sword
              the map of the world
under curtains of air

                                    Longer eyelids
In the opposite room
                    A cloud sinks

                              Night emerges in a flash of lightning
                                    —Pierre Reverdy,
                                    "Birth of the Storm"

 hat do you hear in those white spaces?

Imagine what they might be saying; write it down if you like.

Silence is more musical than any song.
—Christina Rossetti

Choose a poem from your anthology composed of many white spaces. Try to "read" these silences: First read the text out loud, treating the white space in the same way you would blank measures in sheet music. Then ask yourself what these silences contain: What are they accentuating, what are they prolonging?

Day 123

If you want, translate them into words, gestures, music, or graphics.

True silence is the rest of the mind; it is to the spirit
what sleep is to the body, nourishment and refreshment.
—William Penn

W

rite a poem that
celebrates silence: a
poem in which the words (and their layout) incorporate the use of silence.

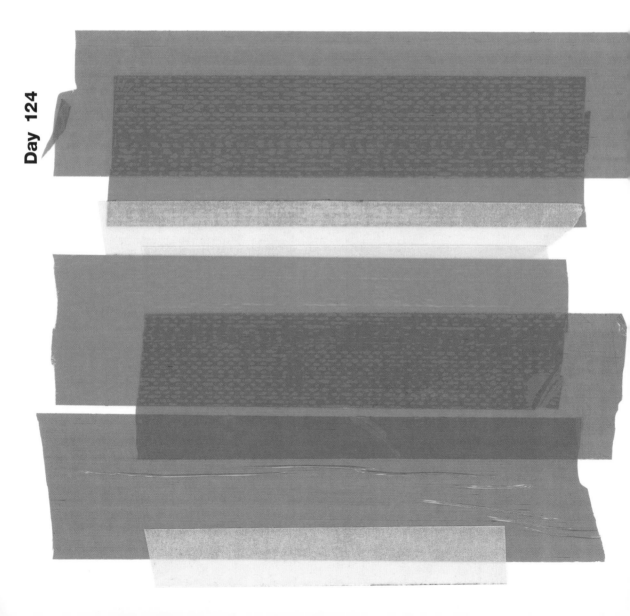

The right word may be effective, but no word was ever
as effective as a rightly timed pause.
—Mark Twain

There are other ways of dividing up or giving rhythm to a text:

the ellipsis:

Sleep softly . . . eagle forgotten . . . under the stone.
Time has its way with you there, and the clay has its own.
—Vachel Lindsay,
from "The Eagle That Is Forgotten"

the dash:

These are the days when Birds come back—
A very few—a Bird or two—
To take a backward look.

—Emily Dickinson,
from "These are the days when Birds come back"

and other kinds of punctuation dispersed within the text.

Write a poem using these different tools. You can write a poem
on breathing, speed,
or slowness . . .

Fill a space in a beautiful way.
—Georgia O'Keefe

Three boxes

Compose a text that will fit inside these three boxes.

Poetry is an orphan of silence. The words never quite
equal the experience behind them.
—Charles Simic

Cut a long, narrow strip of paper.
Write or draw onto it the first word or
image that pops into your head. Follow
that with another word or image that
comes to you, and so on . . . The goal is
to write as fast as possible, using both
sides of the strip of paper. Repeat the
activity several times during the course
of the day.

Day 127

Poems are attempts to prove the realness of the world,
and of myself in this world, by establishing the realness
of my relation to it.
—Ted Hughes

Take your texts from yesterday. Write them on another sheet of paper (or type them into your computer) and play with the placement of the words—move them around, discover their rhythm . . . You can modify your original texts by deleting or repeating certain passages (or words).

Poetry is the time during which the thought of death is suspended.
—Georges Perros

Invent some "writing spaces" and explore them . . .

The forms of things unknown, the poet's pen
Turns them to shapes, and gives to airy nothing
A local habitation and a name.
—William Shakespeare

Day 130

You
  faced
    death
      more
       than
        a
         hundred
          times
          you
           don't
            know
             what
             life
             is
              —Guillaume Apollinaire,
                from "Cornflower 1917"

Take a sheet of paper. Write in diagonal. Don't know what to write? Don't worry; the movement of your hand will guide and inspire the writing.

Take a sheet of paper. Fold it in half. Mark the fold well. Now write under and over the fold. What does the fold evoke in you: A boundary? A path? A thread?

Day 131

All of poetry is a drawing.
—Mahmoud Darwish

Cut a strip of paper about two inches wide. Place it vertically on a table. Start writing on the bottom, and work your way up . . .

Poetry is ordinary language raised to the nth power.
—Paul Engle

Day 133

Explore other departure points for writing: Start from the center of the page, for example,

or try writing in zigzags, circles, squares, or from right to left, etc.

Poetry lifts the veil from the hidden beauty of the world, and makes familiar objects be as if they were not familiar.
—Percy Bysshe Shelley

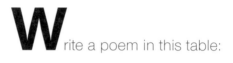

Write a poem in this table:

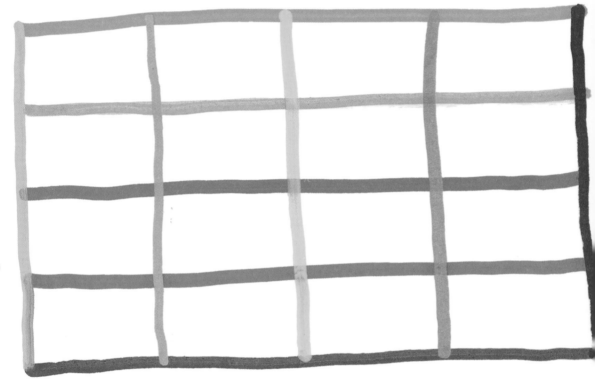

A pointer: you don't have to start from the upper left-hand box!

If you're at a loss for words, begin with the following words:

when	there	bus
window	waiting	armchairs
crossing		

Poetry gives you permission to feel.
—James Autry

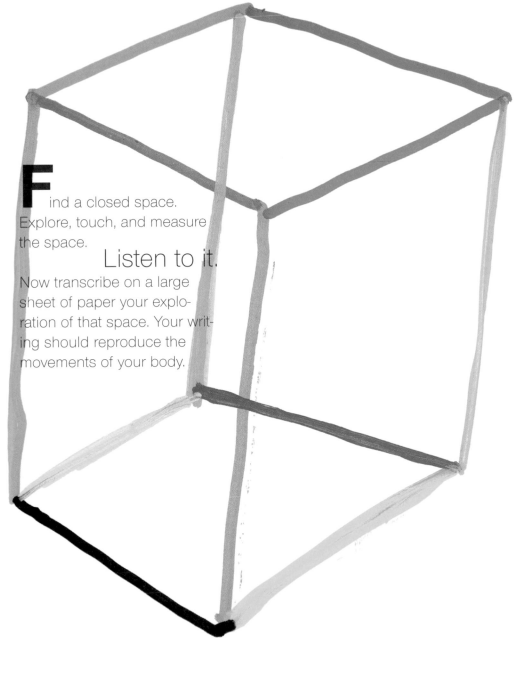

Find a closed space.
Explore, touch, and measure
the space.
Listen to it.
Now transcribe on a large
sheet of paper your exploration of that space. Your writing should reproduce the
movements of your body.

Day 135

You will find poetry nowhere unless you bring some of
it with you.
—Joseph Joubert

C hoose a poem for each room of your apartment or house.

To have great poets there must be great audiences too.
—Walt Whitman

Place some of your poems in the outside world: Hang them onto a clothes line, post them in the stairwell of your building or on a tree in the park, tack them to a public bulletin board . . . Take a photo or record the reactions to this poetic undertaking . . .

Day 137

Poetry is an echo, asking a shadow to dance.
—Carl Sandburg

Cut a small piece out of a newspaper, sheet music, phone book, or
dictionary. Turn it upside down so you
can't read what's printed on it. Now
write between or over the lines. This is a
way of creating a new path, of laying
claim to your writing.

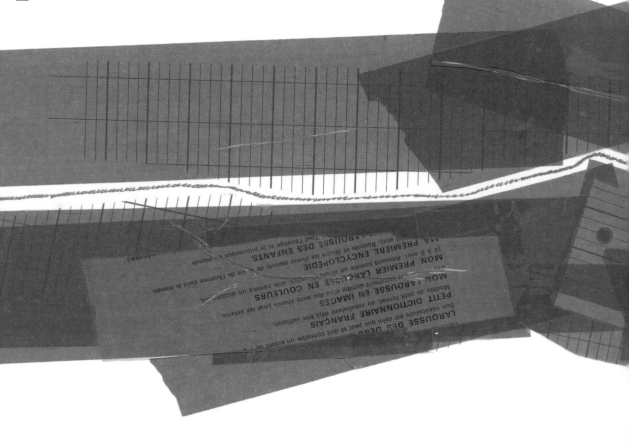

Poetry is boned with ideas, nerved and blooded with
emotions, all held together by the delicate, tough skin
of words.
—Paul Engle

Cut out twenty little pieces of
paper of varying sizes. Place them all in
front of you and write something on
each one. What you write doesn't have
to be consistent. Now mix up all the
pieces and compose a text by assem-
bling them. Feel free to delete or
add words to the ones you
already wrote . . .

Day 139

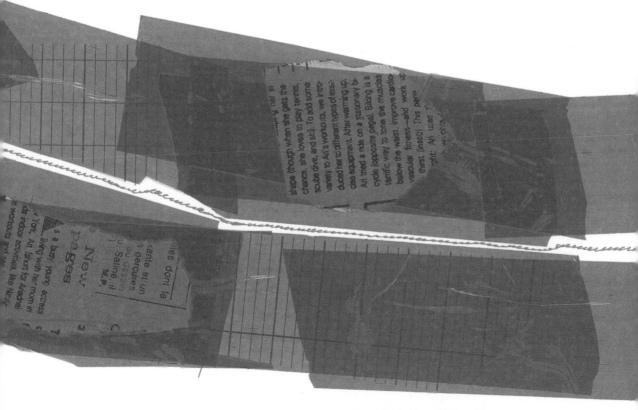

Painting is silent poetry, and poetry is a speaking picture.
—Simonides

Writing in big spaces: Write on a blank canvas, the back of a poster, or on the wall (why not?). Use a writing instrument that you wouldn't normally use, such as a thick marker, or a paint-brush. Let the movements of your hand inspire your choice of words . . .

Day 140

Take a photograph of your work as a keepsake.

A poem is meant to be read and read again and again, to be run through the mind until it is part of the mind, until the mind recites it as it recites itself.

—C. K. Williams

Choose a poem and ask a friend to read it out loud with you.

Try several methods: split it up, read it simultaneously, etc.

Work on your delivery, your breathing, and the harmonies.

Note any comments here.

Poetry is creative expression; poetry is constructive expression.
—Sir Herbert Read

Poem, redux

Choose a poem from this book. Cut it up, mix up all the fragments, eliminate some at your will, and re-compose. In sum: Create a new version of the poem from the old one.

A truncated poem

Write a text (narrative, descriptive, poetic, or philosophical—the choice is yours). Now cut out the beginning and end of the sentences (or just the beginning, or just the end, if you prefer.) A new text within the text will emerge . . .

Poetry is thoughts that breathe, and words that burn.
—Thomas Gray

Write a poem using the headlines cut out of a newspaper and fragments of poems from your notebook.

Day 145

Copy some poems of yours that
you dislike. Before you throw them in
the garbage can, jot down their titles in
this space. If you're feeling courageous,
copy your least favorite poem here.

The whole of nature is a metaphor of the human mind.
—Ralph Waldo Emerson

Day 146

The poet William Henry Davies wrote the following in "The Rain":

> I hear leaves drinking rain;
> I hear rich leaves on top
> Giving the poor beneath
> Drop after drop;
> 'Tis a sweet noise to hear
> These green leaves drinking near.

What do you hear when the rain is falling?

Poetry is the language in which man explores his own
amazement.
—Christopher Fry

Is my shadow my shadow?
—Jean-Claude Renard

Poetry often questions the obvious.
You, too, can question reality.

Is night truly night?

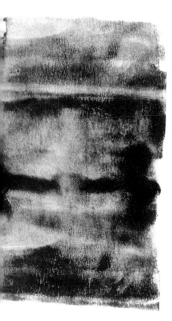

Is silence silent?

Poetry is not a civilizer, rather the reverse, for great
poetry appeals to the most primitive instincts.
—Robinson Jeffers

Kids like picking their nose.
In class, some of them would eat what
they had found:
it was salty and not altogether unpleasant.
—Daniel Biga,
"Picking One's Nose"

Now it's your turn to write a short
text on the following themes:
biting one's nails
eating a piece of candy
sharpening a pencil
getting a haircut

Poetry is the impish attempt to paint
the colour of the wind.
—Maxwell Bodenheim

Here is a fragment of the poem "Primroses" by William Carlos Williams:

Yellow, yellow, yellow, yellow!
It is not a color.
It is summer!
It is the wind on a willow,
the lap of waves, the shadow
under a bush, a bird, a bluebird,
three herons, a dead hawk
rotting on a pole—
Clear yellow!

Now it's your turn: Think about the color yellow,

noting the images,
words, and feelings that it inspires in you.

Mere color, unspoiled by meaning, and unallied with definite form, can speak to the soul in a thousand different ways.
—Oscar Wilde

How about yellow, green, black, or beige . . . ? Choose a color today,

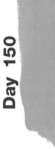

Day 150

What is pink? A rose is pink
By the fountain's brink.
What is red? A poppy's red
In its barley bed.
What is blue? The sky is blue
Where the clouds float through.
What is white? A swan is white
Sailing in the light.
What is yellow? Pears are yellow,
Rich and ripe and mellow.
What is green? The grass is green,
With small flowers between.
What is violet? Clouds are violet
In the summer twilight.
What is orange? Why, an orange,
Just an orange!
                    —Christina Rossetti,
                    "What Is Pink?"

and like yesterday, write what it inspires in you.

Do you remember this popular nursery rhyme?

This is the house that Jack built.

This is the malt
That lay in the house that Jack built.

This is the rat,
That ate the malt
That lay in the house that Jack built.

This is the cat,
That killed the rat,
That ate the malt
That lay in the house that Jack built . . .
—Mother Goose

Day 151

Now it's your turn! Start with the first line and create a modern take on this Mother Goose rhyme.

Poetry has no goal other than itself.
—Charles Baudelaire

What does the wind say when it's silent?
What does the wind's silence say?
—Claude Roy

Can you respond to the following
questions with a poem?

Logic dictates that a stone is mute.
Love dictates that it's merely afraid to speak.
—Alain Bosque

The rain plays a little sleep song on our roof at night
—Langston Hughes,
from "April Rain Song"

Give a voice to a crumb, an empty bottle, a shoelace, a potato . . .

Day 153

And then I pressed the shell
Close to my ear
And listened well,
And straightway like a bell
Came low and clear
The slow, sad murmur of the distant seas,
Whipped by an icy breeze
Upon a shore
Wind-swept and desolate.

—James Stephens,
from "The Shell"

Place an object in your hand and listen to it. Listen. What is it saying? What language is it speaking? If it's mute, give it a voice.

Day 154

Poetry is creating something we will never see.
—Gerardo Diego

The French poet Pierre Coran "interviewed" a calculator, a flute, and a spoon.

Now it's your turn. Interview one of your nightmares, or a piece of dust under your bed.

Invent a new language.
Write the first poem in this unknown language.

Day 156

What is a poet if not a decoder, a decipherer?
—Charles Baudelaire

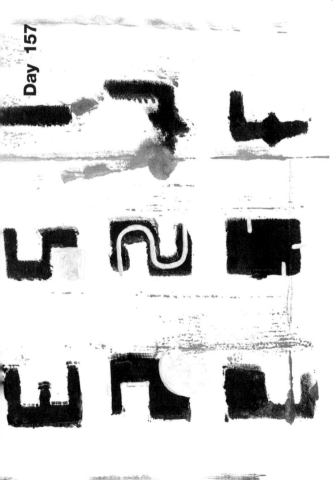

Here is a poem written in a Scottish dialect. Read it out loud (don't worry, no one is listening!) and let it speak to you. Now, translate it into words you know. It doesn't matter if you don't know all the words: Guess, imagine, or invent their meaning . . .

Wee, sleeket, cowran, tim'rous beastie,
O, what panic's in thy breastie!
Thou need na start awa sae hasty,
Wi' bickering brattle!
I wad be laith to rin an' chase thee,
Wi' murd'ring pattle!

—Robert Burns,
from "To a Mouse"

Listen to a poem in a language you don't understand (you can find some at this website: www.lyrikline.org). Listen to it several times, allow images to form in your mind, and let words translate these images. Now translate the poem you heard.

The force of a language does not consist of rejecting
what is foreign but of swallowing it.
—Johann Wolfgang von Goethe

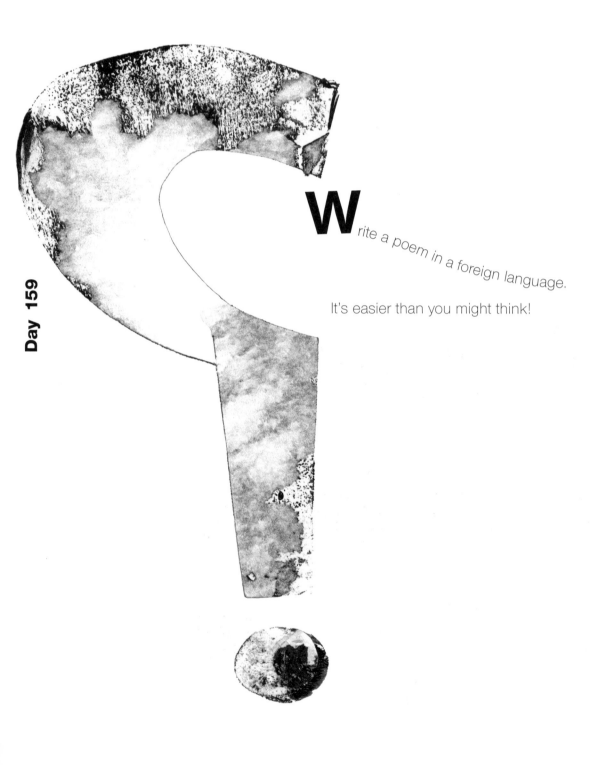

Write a poem in a foreign language.

It's easier than you might think!

Poetry creates its own autonomous world, and what
that world asks from us it also answers within us.
—Edward Hirsch

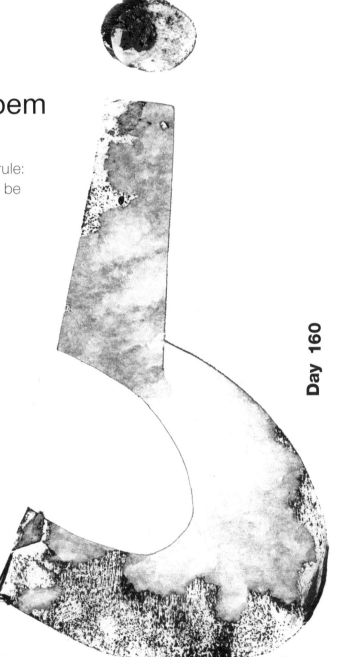

A question-mark poem

Today's exercise has only one rule:
Every sentence of your poem must be
a question.

Day 160

Language that tells us, through a more or less emotional
reaction, something that cannot be said.
—E. A. Robinson

A dialogue poem

Write a poem consisting of
questions and answers.

The past and present wilt—I have fill'd
  them, emptied them.
And proceed to fill my next fold of the
  future.

Listener up there! what have you to
  confide to me?
Look in my face while I snuff the sidle
  of evening,
(Talk honestly, no one else hears you,
  and I stay only a minute longer.)

Do I contradict myself?
Very well then I contradict myself,
(I am large, I contain multitudes.)
                    —Walt Whitman,
              from "Song of Myself"

An affirmative poem

Write a poem consisting of questions and answers, like you did yesterday. This time, erase the questions, leaving only the answers.

Doubt equals writing.
—Marguerite Duras

Do you have doubts?
Of what?
Why?
Write your answer in a poem.
Perhaps.

Today's objective:

Read a collection of poems published
around a year ago. First, leaf through the
poems and pick out some words or fragments that catch your eye and copy
them here. Now experiment with several
new ways of reading these texts together.
(This exercise is similar to the ones you
completed on Days 110 and 111).

Day 164

No poem will be so great, so noble, so truly worthy of the name of poem, than one written uniquely for the pleasure of writing a poem.

—Charles Baudelaire

Read the last few poems that you wrote. Were they written "for the pleasure of writing a poem"? Write about what you discovered these last few weeks about writing, YOUR writing.

An exclamatory poem

Today's poem must consist of exclamatory sentences.

Heart, we will forget him!
You and I—tonight!
You may forget the warmth he gave—
I will forget the light!

When you have done, pray tell me
That I may straight begin!
Haste! lest while you're lagging
I remember him!

—Emily Dickinson,
from "Heart, we will forget him"

A negative poem

Write a poem composed of negative statements.

I no longer snicker I smile no more
I no longer lower my eyes nor lift them high
I don't even rub them I can't sleep
I keep watch like a shadowless stone
—Philippe Soupault

Day 167

Write a "contradictory" poem.

I do not look at things, and things look at me;
I do not move, and the floor under my feet moves me
—Peter Handke,
from "The Wrong Way Around"

Poetry is all nouns and verbs.
—Marianne Moore

Add some new words to the dictionary. It's easy—just think of a word and use it as a noun, adjective, verb, adverb, etc.

They garreted me, microscoped, marauded, test-tubed,
gutted, trapped, badgered, trapped-trapped,
they fundamentalized me, hastened me, ambushed me
(that's for tomorrow!), pimpam, my brain, my brain!
—Jean-Pierre Verheggen

A futuristic poem

In today's poem, all your verbs will be in the future tense.

Tomorrow at dawn, just as the countryside is set alight, I will set off.
I know you will wait for me.
I will travel by forest, I will travel by mountain.
I can't keep my distance from you any longer.

I will walk with my eyes not veering from my thoughts
Seeing not a thing, hearing not a noise,
Alone, unknown, hands clasped and back bent,
Sad, and the day shall for me be as night.

I shall not gaze at the evening's golden hues,
Nor at the distant vessels sailing to Harfleur.
And once I arrive, on your tomb I will place
A wreath of green holly and blooming heather.

—Victor Hugo,
"Tomorrow, at Dawn"

I could no more define poetry than a terrier can define
a rat.
—A. E. Houseman

A hypothetical poem

Today's poem will be in the
conditional tense, obviously.

Day 171

Wild Nights! Wild Nights!
Were I with thee,
Wild nights should be
our luxury!

Futile the winds
To a heart in port, —
Done with the compass,
Done with the chart.

Rowing in Eden!
Ah! the sea!
Might I but moor
To-night in thee!

—Emily Dickinson,
"Wild Nights"

Day 172

Find a poem that combines many
tenses—past, present, future, conditional.
Or write your own.

I would define, in brief, the Poetry of words
as the Rhythmical Creation of Beauty.
—Edgar Allen Poe

Day 173

Read out loud this picturesque
song-poem, "Break, Break, Break," by
Alfred, Lord Tennyson:

Break, break, break,
On thy cold gray stones, O Sea!
And I would that my tongue could utter
The thoughts that arise in me.

O, well for the fisherman's boy,
That he shouts with his sister at play!
O, well for the sailor lad,
That he sings in his boat on the bay!

And the stately ships go on
To their haven under the hill;
But O for the touch of a vanished hand,
And the sound of a voice that is still!

Break, break, break,
At the foot of thy crags, O Sea!
But the tender grace of a day that is dead
Will never come back to me.

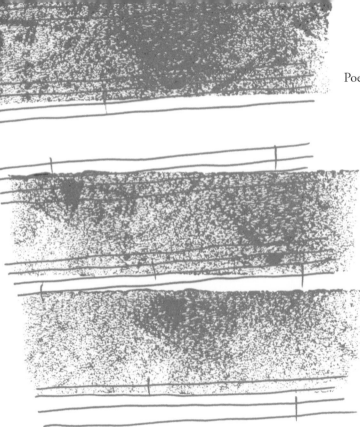

Poetry is plucking at the heartstrings, and making music with them.
—Dennis Gabor

Add some song lyrics to your poetry anthology. What is the difference between poetry and lyrics?

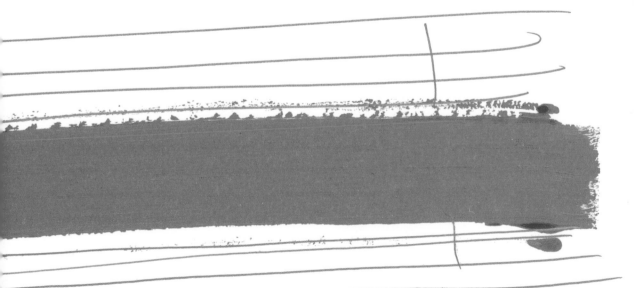

Poetry is like a piece of music: you have to hear it to judge it.
—Voltaire

Try to put one of your poems to music. Record or note here the music you composed.

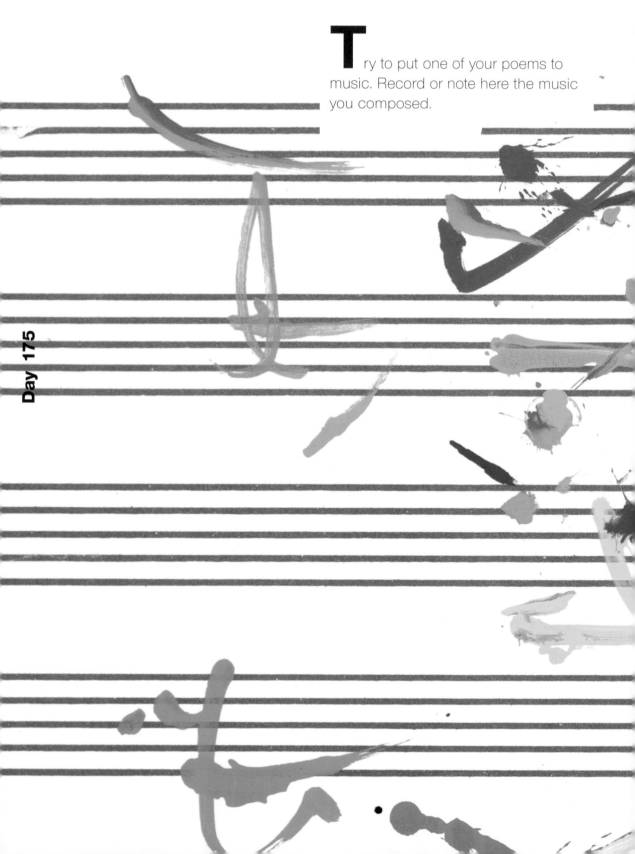

Add some poems to your anthology that were inspired by music (start with poems entitled "Song," of which there are many).

Day 176

My poetry, I think, has become the way of my giving
out what music is within me.
—Countee Cullen

Listen to a song you like several
times. Now write a poem echoing this
music.

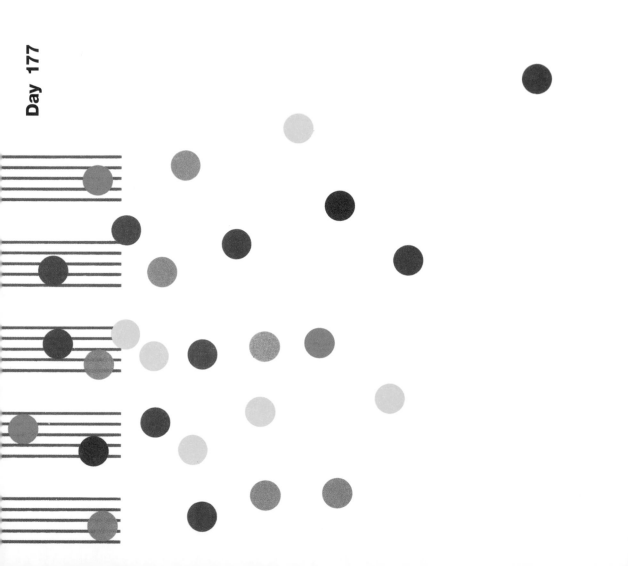

A hidden poem

Unveil the poem, or poems, within this text. To do so, take a black marker and start covering the lines, leaving only the fragments you will use to compose your poem.

. . . deceptive detours by way of elementary truths: what is war? What absurd, unbearable reason—more intense than the love of their children—makes humans accept losing everything, including their own lives? And further-more, what is cruelty? How is it that one group is chosen as the enemy? [. . .] Children know that adults, like themselves, lack answers to these questions [. . .] Based on my own experiences as a child during wartime, the separation described in *Flon-Flon & Musette* shouldn't be interpreted as a purely physical and emotional separation. The thorny hedges that suddenly appear in the story symbolize the arbitrary nature of taboo, the system of vicious selection.

In *White Rose*, Roberto Innocenti, like Elzbieta, does some soul-searching and draws on his own experiences. "In *White Rose*," he says, "I had the impression that I was an old man looking for his childhood. It surpassed my interest in History. Everything was linked to personal memories, the memory of the war I witnessed when I was little." In it, the reader is struck by its extremely realistic depiction of war, World War II, notably the concentration camps. The title itself alludes to a youthful anti-Nazi resistance group, *Die weisse Rose*; the illustrations are marked by an almost documentary precision, bordering on photographic (particularly the image of the little boy, arms raised, being stopped by soldiers in what is obviously the Warsaw ghetto). But by moving from first to third person—the voice of the little girl to that of the narrator searching for truth—the story incorporates both a poetic dimension and a very powerful emotional charge. Tomi Ungerer, in *Otto: Autobiographie eines Teddybären*, adopts a different, more traditional, approach. Whereas Elzbieta and Roberto Innocenti strive to understand a childhood experience through images engraved in their memory and with an adult sensibility, Tomi Ungerer tells a cautionary tale in the imaginary voice of a teddy bear . . .

Day 178

N.B.: Feel free to change the order of the words, add some text, or repeat certain words.

Each memorable verse of a true poet has two or three times the written content.
—Alfred de Musset

H

ide a poem within a text. To do this, cut a poem into fragments that you will integrate in a text on a subject of your choice (it can be a newspaper article, economic analysis, botany report—anything . . .). This activity is the inverse of the one you did yesterday. The choice of poem to conceal is up to you.

Fragments came floating into his mind like bits of wood drifting down a stream, and he fished them out and put them together.
—Elizabeth Gray Vining

Poetry is a packsack of invisible keepsakes.
—Carl Sandburg

Day 180

Choose a poem (a long one) and uncover the poem or poems that are hidden inside it. Proceed as you did on Day 178.

A poem is an instant of lucidity in which the entire
organism participates.
—Charles Simic

Take one of your poems and cut
it up into fragments to obtain several
different poems (of various lengths).

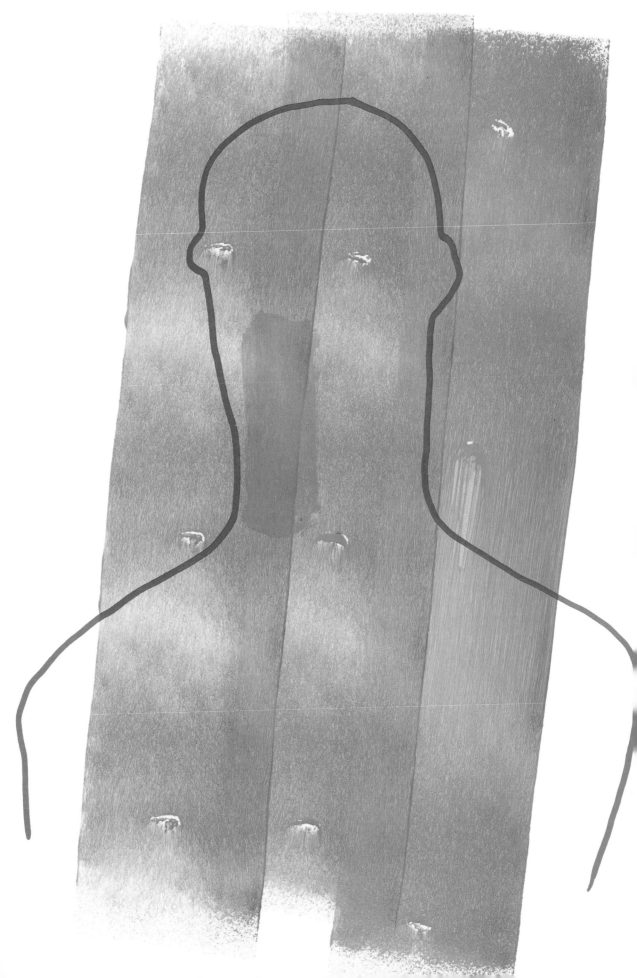

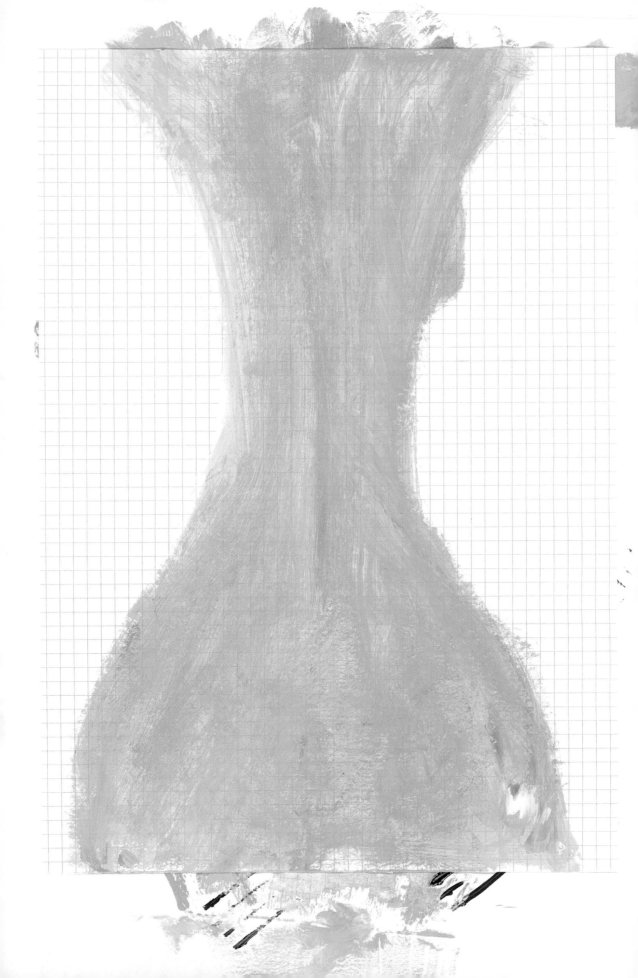

Take an account of your more than 180 days of writing. To begin, reread some of your texts. Choose one and rework it: Lengthen it, reformat it, and read it out loud. Compare the original version with your new version. Make a note of your changes.

Day 182

A poem is a new beginning.
—André du Bouchet

Day 183

Redo an activity from this journal that you particularly enjoyed.

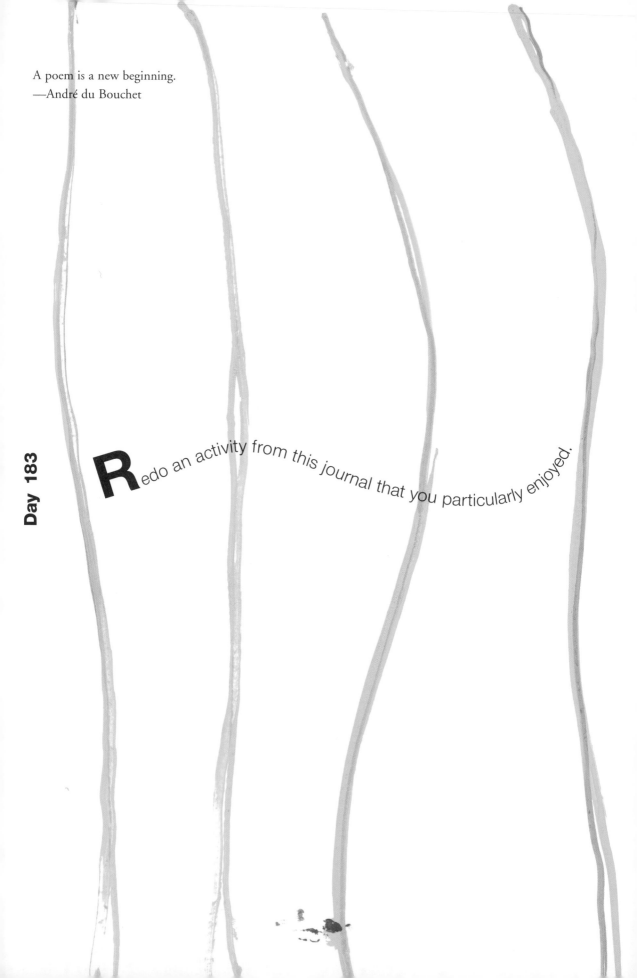

A common refrain . . .

Start with a word or phrase of your choice and draw it out by repeating it, modifying it, or moving it around. In the following excerpt, that word is "rapping."

Once upon a midnight dreary, while I pondered weak and weary,
Over many a quaint and curious volume of forgotten lore,
While I nodded, nearly napping, suddenly there came a tapping,
As of some one gently rapping, rapping at my chamber door.
" 'Tis some visitor," I muttered, "tapping at my chamber door.
Only this, and nothing more."

—Edgar Allen Poe,
from "The Raven"

I know [ten-dollar words] all right. But there are older and simpler and better words, and those are the ones I use.
—Ernest Hemingway

Play with the various levels of language, mixing up formal language with everyday language, precious words with street words.
What do you end up with?

Take some time to look around you,
at the everyday objects of life: the surface
of a table, the molding of a ceiling, or
the veins of a leaf . . . try to decode their
messages.

Day 186

The poet doesn't write; no, he listens.
—Jean-Marie Barnaud

Day 187

Read this poem out loud, first in a closed room, then outside. Let the sounds speak to you, let the words vibrate through your ears. Can you hear the sound of the sea?

The sea awoke at midnight from its sleep,
And round the pebbly beaches far and wide
I heard the first wave of the rising tide
Rush onward with uninterrupted sweep;
A voice out of the silence of the deep,
A sound mysteriously multiplied
As of a cataract from the mountain's side,
Or roar of winds upon a wooded steep.
So comes to us at times, from the unknown
And inaccessible solitudes of being,
The rushing of the sea-tides of the soul;
And inspirations, that we deem our own,
Are some divine of foreshadowing and foreseeing
Of things beyond our reason or control.
                    —Henry Wadsworth Longfellow,
                        "The Sound of the Sea"

Keep it simple and make it visual seems to be
the best idea.
—Hugo Williams

Place your hands under cold, running water and close your eyes.
Try to describe how it feels to you, and the images it conjures up.

Day 188

You cannot depend on your eyes when your imagination
is out of focus.
—Mark Twain

Today, you're going to write in the dark. Prepare a sheet of paper and a pen, or turn on your computer. Then turn off all the lights in the room, or blindfold yourself. Now write.

Poetry is to prose as dancing is to walking.
—John Wain

Choose a poem (either
one you've already written or
one you copied into your anthology)
and dance to it. That's right: Interpret
the words by moving your body.
Don't be shy—no one's
watching!

The dance is a poem of which each movement is a word.
—Mata Hari

Clear a space where you can dance freely.

In the corner, place several sheets of paper and something to write with. Now begin: DANCE, invent a language using the movements of your body. When an emotion, word, or image inspires you, jot it down quickly on a sheet of paper. Allow the sheets of paper to fall where they may, dispersed haphazardly around the dance floor . . .

Using either a stick or your fingers (whichever you prefer), write

a poem in the sand or soil before the wind, or the sea, sweeps it away . . .

If you want to leave a trace, photograph it.

Day 192

The windows of my poetry are wide open on the
boulevards
—Blaise Cendrars

Day 193

O pen your window and let poetry in (or out).

They are rattling breakfast plates in basement kitchens,
And along the trampled edges of the street
I am aware of the damp souls of housemaids
Sprouting despondently at area gates.

The brown waves of fog toss up to me
Twisted faces from the bottom of the street,
And tear from a passer-by with muddy skirts
An aimless smile that hovers in the air
And vanishes along the level of the roofs.

—T. S. Eliot,
"Morning at the Window"

The job of the poet is not to tell you it is raining; the job of the poet is to make rain.
—Paul Valéry

What is the weather like today?

Shower shower shower shower shower
rain O rain O rain! O rain O rain O rain!
waterdrops waterdrops waterdrops waterdrops
—Raymond Queneau

Breathes there the man, with soul so dead, who never
to himself hath said, this is my own, my native land!
—Sir Walter Scott

Day 195

Write a new national
(but not nationalist) anthem.

A poem in the infinitive

In today's poem, all the verbs are in the infinitive tense. What effect does it have?

To slither with the snake
to slip between the lines
to roar with the panthers
to interpret the slightest sign
to lounge in the sands
to bond in the grasses
to blossom with all one's being.
—Michel Butor

Day 196

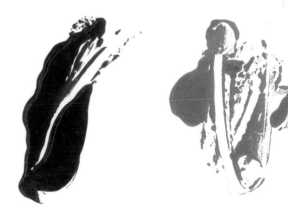

A poem is always the energy of a voice.
—Zéno Bianu

Take the poem from yesterday. Conjugate the verbs in the infinitive tense by introducing an "I," a "you," a "he," or a "she."

A poem in the imperative

Today's exercise is easy: write a poem composed of verbs in the imperative tense.

Day 198

Poet, never chase the dream.
Laugh yourself, and turn away.
Mask your hunger; let it seem
Small matter if he come or stay;
But when he nestles in your hand at last,
Close up your fingers tight and hold him fast.
—Robert Graves,
from "A Pinch of Salt"

It is well to remember that grammar is common
speech formulated.
—William Somerset Maugham

Jean-Michel Maulpoix wrote:

When it comes to grammar books,
what I like most of all are the examples:
short sentences, either written from
scratch or lifted from books, removed
from their context and thrown together
like the ramblings of a deranged writer.

Take a grammar book (or a foreign
language primer). Pick out some
sample sentences. Now put them
all together and find a poetic
connection between them.

The greater part of the world's troubles are due to
questions of grammar.
—Michel de Montaigne

Choose some grammatical con-
straints for yourself in today's lesson.
For example, you can decide to write a
poem composed solely of nouns
(without their articles), verbs in the
infinitive, or adjectives.

Day 200

True poetry lives outside the law.
—Georges Bataille

Words on the move

Take one of your poems and pick out a fragment of several lines. Change the order of the words; you can attempt several different versions. (You can also choose any other fragment of text: a newspaper article, a passage from a story, or a song . . .).

Come, little boy, and rock asleep;
Sing lullaby and be thou still
—Nicholas Breton

Isn't a lullaby a gentle, rhyming song sung to children to help them fall asleep? Not always. Many authors and poets have played with this genre. Search for some examples on the Internet.

Now the day is done,
Now the shepherd sun
Drives his white flocks from the sky;
Now the flowers rest
On their mother's breast,
Hushed by her low lullaby.
—Louisa May Alcott,
from "Lullaby"

Day 202

Golden slumbers kiss your eyes,
Smiles awake you when you rise.
Sleep, pretty wantons, do not cry,
And I will sing a lullaby.
—Thomas Dekker

Day 203

Write a lullaby. Listen to its melody in your mind.

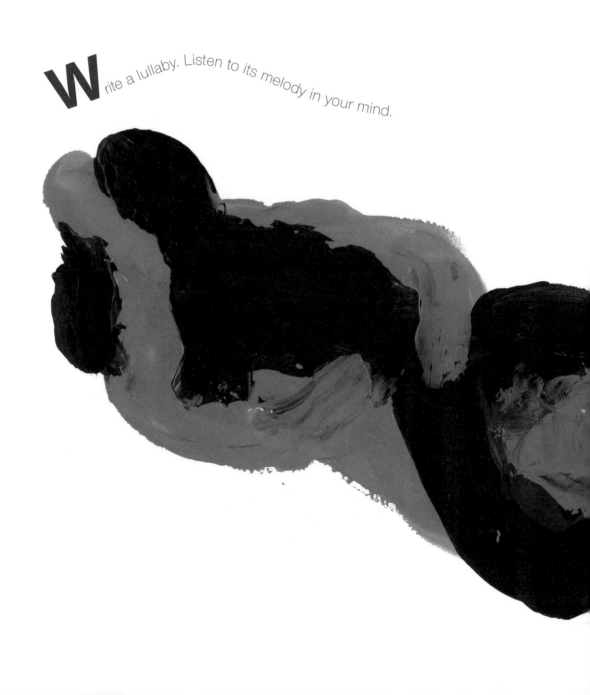

Again and again, however we know the landscape of love.
—Rainer Maria Rilke

Add several love poems to your anthology.

An old silver church in a forest
Is my love for you.
The trees around it
Are words that I have stolen from your heart.
An old silver bell, the last smile you gave,
Hangs at the top of my church.
It rings only when you come through the forest
And stand beside it.
And then, it has no need for ringing,
For your voice takes its place.
—Maxwell Bodenheim,
"Poet to His Love"

Writing isn't living. Perhaps it's surviving.
—Blaise Cendrars

A prescription poem

Write a poem inspired by the leaflets included in a box of medicine.

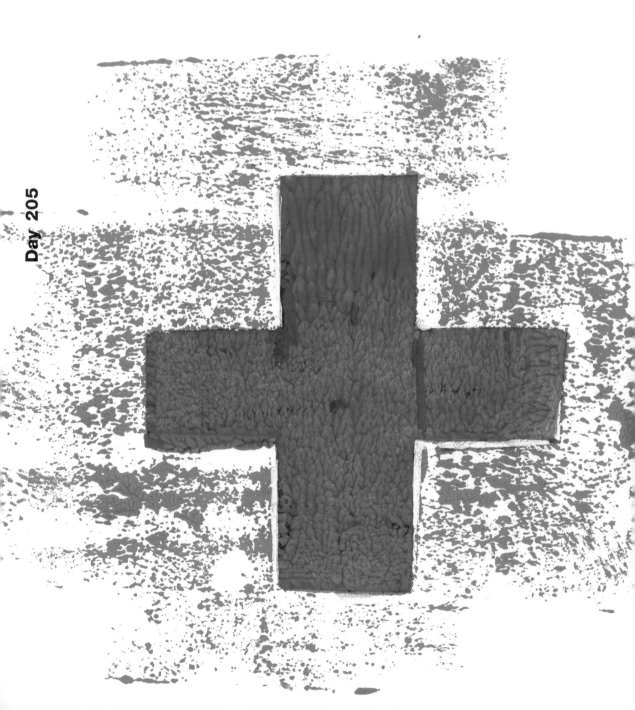

My hand is the extension of the thinking process—
the creative process.
—Tadao Ando

Day 206

Write a poem in prose about your hand. To begin, look at your hand from every possible angle, rub it against a rough surface, then against something very soft. Wiggle your fingers, crack your knuckles, make sweeping movements in the air.
Now write.

The hand is the organ of language.
—Valère Novarina

Place your hand flat on a sheet of paper, with your fingers slightly spread apart. Trace the contours of your hand. Now write in the space. Imagine that you are tattooing a poem on the back of your hand.

There is no instinct like that of the heart.
—Lord Byron

Write a poem in which the word
"love" appears several times. Keep in
mind that it doesn't necessarily have to
be a love poem!

Ink runs from the corners of my mouth.
There is no happiness like mine.
I have been eating poetry.
—Mark Strand

A gourmet poem

Transform your favorite recipe into a
poem.

To make this condiment, your poet begs
The pounded yellow of two hard-boiled
    eggs;
Two boiled potatoes, passed through
    kitchen sieve,
Smoothness and softness to the salad give.

Let onion atoms lurk within the bowl,
And, half suspected, animate the whole.
Of mordant mustard add a single spoon,
Distrust the condiment that bites so soon;
But deem it not, thou man of herbs, a
    fault,
To add a double quantity of salt
              —Sydney Smith,
        from "Recipe for a Salad"

Day 209

If food is poetry, is not poetry also food?
—Joyce Carol Oates

Words to eat

Chocolate, strawberries, peaches, and apple pie ... appetizing words, mouthwatering memories, and delectable images. Serve up a savory text.

If thou tastest a crust of bread, thou tastest all the stars and all the heavens
—Robert Browning

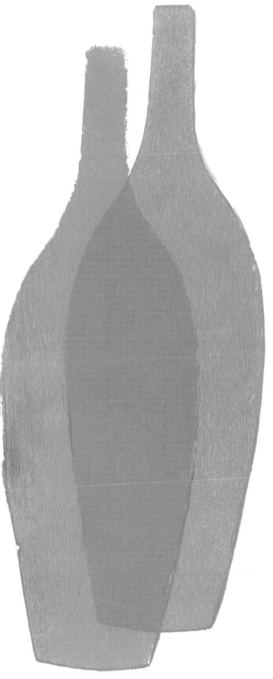

Day 210

One should eat to live, not live to eat.
—Cicero

A diet poem

Invent a "light poem," a 0% poem,
one without any fat or added sugars . . .

Poetry appeals to our eyes as well as our tastebuds. A poem, however simple, can awaken our sensory memory. Read the following poem out loud. Which sense does it evoke? Write your own poem about a hot or cold day.

O wind, rend open the heat,
Cut apart the heat,
Rend it to tatters.
Fruit cannot drop
Through this thick air—
Fruit cannot fall into heat
That presses up and blunts
The points of pears
And rounds the grapes.
Cut the heat—
Plough through it,
Turning it on either side
Of your path.
—H. D., "Heat"

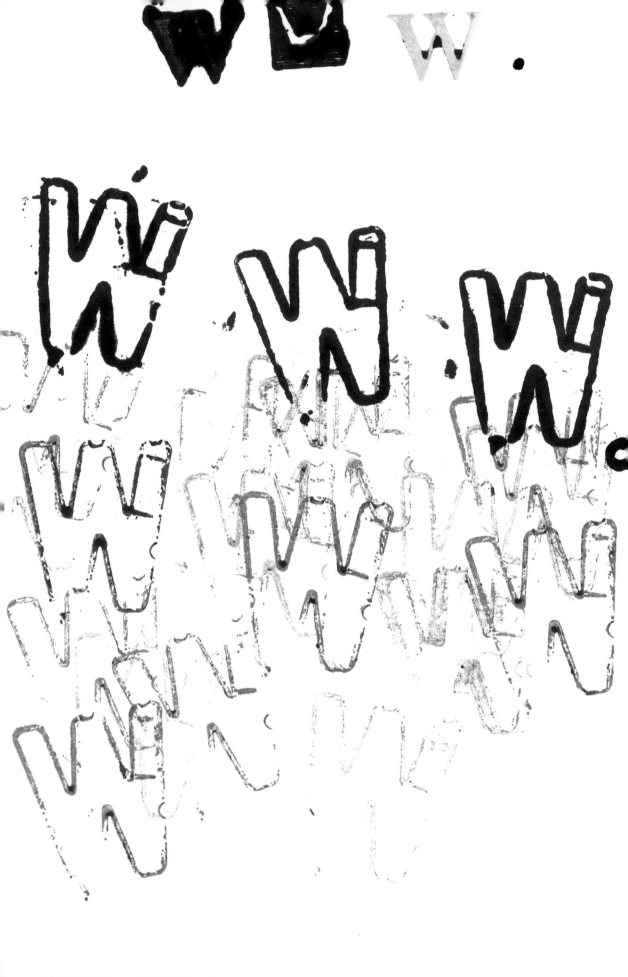

All the fun is in how you say the thing.
—Robert Frost

Which poem do you associate with a glass of apple juice, or a Coca-Cola? Look through your anthology or on the Internet.

Day 213

At first it was a study. I wrote of silences and nights.
I noted the inexpressable. I fixed vertigoes.
—Arthur Rimbaud

Blaise Cendrars wrote "elastic
poems" and Louis Calaferte wrote
"scalding poems."
What if you were to invent
"waterproof poems"
or "transparent poems"?
Or, how about a
"chewing-gum poem"?

Poets write odes to objects they love or revere. One famous ode is "Ode to a Grecian Urn," by John Keats.

> O Attic shape! Fair attitude! with brede
> Of marble men and maidens overwrought,
> With forest branches and the trodden weed;
> Thou, silent form, dost tease us out of thought
> As doth eternity [. . .]

Many modern poets write odes to ordinary objects, like socks or pens. Can you write an ode to a toothbrush, to your sneakers, to a window, or your cellular phone?

Day 215

One should love best what is nearest and most inter-
woven with one's life.
—William Butler Yeats

Everyday poetry

Going to the post office,
taking out the garbage,
making your bed,
cleaning your room,
mopping the kitchen floor . . .

These are all ordinary, everyday
chores. But what do they become
in poetry?

A topical poem

Cut out a headline or news item
from the newspaper. Transform it into a
poem by breaking up the text, and
either deleting, repeating, or repositio-
ning the words.

Armed
with a 9 mm semi-automatic
and a .45-calibre
a lone gunman
opened fire

alone
a gunman opened fire
and hit several people
—Patrick Bouvet

Day 217

It is not necessary to write to be a poet. It is necessary
only to be in a state of grace.
—Léon-Paul Fargue

Day 218

A free day.
Finally: a day when you don't have to
write words on paper or type them on
the screen.
Instead, take some time to
look, contemplate, and listen.
Around you.
And inside of you.

Scattered words

During the course of your day, make a note (discreetly) of the words exchanged by strangers on the bus, in the street, or on the radio. Put them all together and acknowledge their poetic value. You can specify, for example, the place or the time at which you heard the various snippets of conversation.

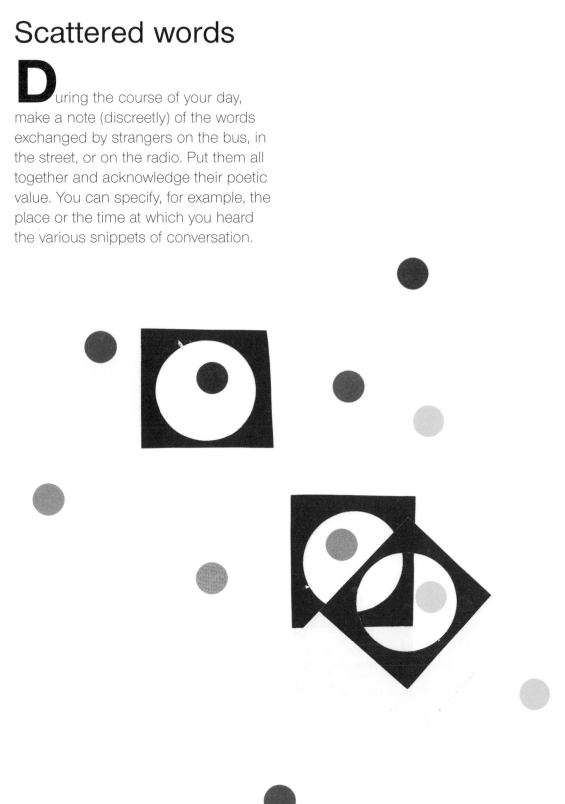

Day 219

Poetry is a matter of life, not just a matter of language.
—Lucille Clifton

W

rite a poem starting with a phrase we utter nearly every day without thinking about it:
Hello, how are you?
What do you do for a living?
It's so hot out today!
Be careful.

A shape poem

Nature has no outline. Imagination has.
—William Blake

Write a poem that takes on a distinct shape. Try to shape it in a way that subtly (or not) relates to the subject of the poem, such as Lewis Carroll's "A Mouse's Tale":

"Fury said to
 a mouse, That
       he met
         in the
          house,
         'Let us
          both go
          to law:
          I will
       prosecute
        you.—
Come, I'll
        take no
        denial;
        We must
         have a
          trial:
              For
           really
          this
           morning
               I've
           nothing
            to do.'
     Said the
     mouse to
    the cur,
      'Such a
        trial,
       dear sir,
    With no
    jury or
  judge,
     would be
      wasting
       our breath.'
        'I'll be
         judge,
         I'll be
         jury,'
    Said
     cunning
       old Fury;
        'I'll try
         the whole
            cause,
            and
          condemn
            you
             to
            death.' "

Day 221

When ideas fail, words come in handy.
—Johann Wolfgang von Goethe

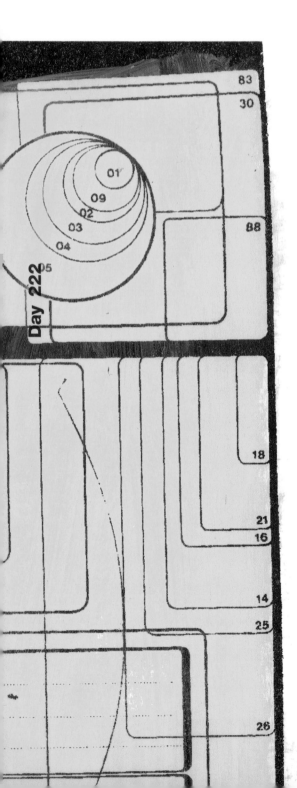

A litany is, literally, a long prayer consisting of a number of petitions, recited in an even tone and constructed in the same way. The French poet Jacques Rebotier wrote some secular litanies. Here are the titles of some of them:

"Litany of the Theatre"
"Litany of Love at First Sight"
"Litany of the Hours"
"Litany of the Streets"

N ow it's your turn. Write a litany of bad excuses, using the following structure:

I'm sorry . . . I . . . because . . .
Example:
I'm sorry, Mom, I couldn't clean my room because the second floor blew away.

The magic in a poem is always accidental.
—Dylan Thomas

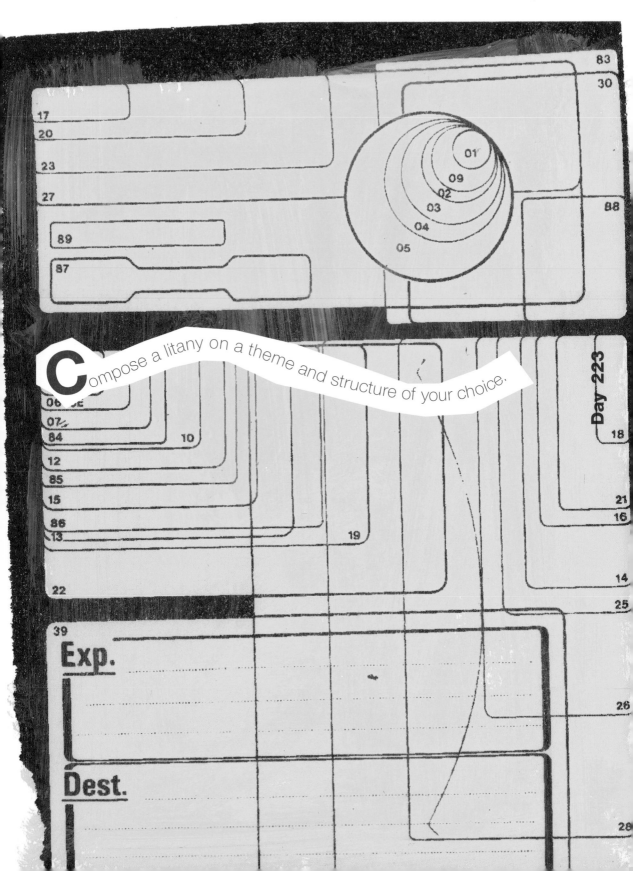

Compose a litany on a theme and structure of your choice.

Happiness is the longing for repetition.
—Milan Kundera

Repetition (of a single word or phrase) is a device used in a large number of poems. Here, for example, is a passage from Shakespeare's *King Lear*:

And my poor fool is hang'd! No, no, no life!
Why should a dog, a horse, a rat, have life,
And thou no breath at all? Thou'lt come no more,
Never, never, never, never, never!

Note how the use of repetition adds emphasis and drama. Find some other examples and add them to your anthology.

The poet conveys his thoughts in festive solemnity on the carriage of rhythm.
—Friedrich Nietzsche

Here are some examples of phrases to repeat:

Beware of . . .

Nobody can say . . .

Small steps . . .

As if . . .

I used to . . .

You will tell them . . .

Choose one of these fragments and repeat it as many times as necessary to compose your poem.

Always and never are two words you should always
remember never to use.
—Wendell Johnson

Compose a poem using the
repetition of a word. For example:

Here
Since
Never
He (or She)
Day
With
Always

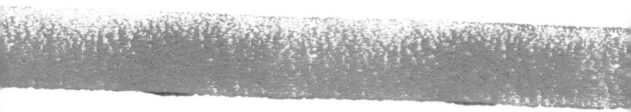

Today's rule:

Each line (or verse) of your poem must
begin with the same syllable (or the
same letter).

Day 227

It is not the simple statement of facts that ushers in freedom; it is the constant repetition of them that has this liberating effect.
—Quentin Crisp

Day 228

Today's poem follows the same principle of repetition, but this time you choose the word or words that will be repeated throughout the poem.

Poetry is always the unexpected.
—Charles Dobzynski

In many poems a form of a word is repeated. Read the following excerpt of "The Cataract of Lodore," by Robert Southey, aloud. What does this kind of repetition convey?

The cataract strong
Then plunges along,
Striking and raging
As if a war waging
Its caverns and rocks among;
Rising and leaping,
Sinking and creeping,
Swelling and sweeping,
Showering and springing,
Flying and flinging,
Writhing and ringing,
Eddying and whisking,
Spouting and frisking,
Turning and twisting,
Around and around
With endless rebound:
Smiting and fighting,
A sight to delight in;
Confounding, astounding,
Dizzying and deafening the ear with its sound.

Poetry is the journal of a sea animal living on land,
wanting to fly in the air.
—Carl Sandburg

Head's up: Raise your eyes and look at the sky (if you're outside!) or the ceiling. Make a note of what you see, in no particular order, and now write, air your thoughts,

but don't go overboard . . .

Microcosm

Take a wooden or cardboard frame. Put it on the ground, hang it on the wall, or lay it on a piece of furniture . . . . Jot down what you see. Now take all your notes and think up a guideline for how to write your next poem.

Day 231

To imagine the unimaginable is the highest use of the imagination.
—Cynthia Ozick

Choose any ordinary object: a button, pencil, potato . . . Touch it, examine it, and ask yourself how you will paint that object using the tools of poetry. How can you communicate what you see, what you feel? Try several times, experiment with different points of view and various expressive styles.

I'm a careless potato, and care not a pin
How into existence I came;
If they planted me drill-wise, or dibbled me in,
To me 'tis exactly the same.
The bean and the pea may more loftily tower,
But I care not a button for them;
Defiance I nod with my beautiful flower
When the earth is hoed up to my stem.
—Thomas Moore,
"The Potato"

Day 233

Describe a place in poetry. Let words replace the images. Capture the colors, sounds, shadows, and movements.

Earth has not anything to show more fair:
Dull would he be of soul who could pass by
A sight so touching in its majesty:
This City now doth, like a garment, wear
The beauty of the morning; silent, bare,
Ships, towers, domes, theatres, and temples lie
Open unto the fields, and to the sky;
All bright and glittering in the smokeless air.
Never did sun more beautifully steep
In his first splendour, valley, rock, or hill;
Ne'er saw I, never felt, a calm so deep!
The river glideth at his own sweet will:
Dear God! the very houses seem asleep;
And all that mighty heart is lying still!

—William Wordsworth,
from "Composed Upon Westminster Bridge,
September 3, 1802"

One's destination is never a place, but a new way of
seeing things.
—Henry Miller

Instead of a postcard, send a poem describing a place you've visited.

I have been in Pennsylvania,
In the Monongahela and Hocking Valleys.

In the blue Susquehanna
On a Saturday morning
I saw a mounted constabulary go by,
I saw boys playing marbles.
Spring and the hills laughed.

—Carl Sandburg,
from "Pennsylvania"

Day 234

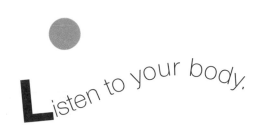

Try to evoke a particular situation:
standing in front of a ticket office, taking
a shower, napping on the beach . . . Make
a note of the sensations, movements,
and impressions of your body in those
moments.

The poet is a liar who always speaks the truth.
—Jean Cocteau

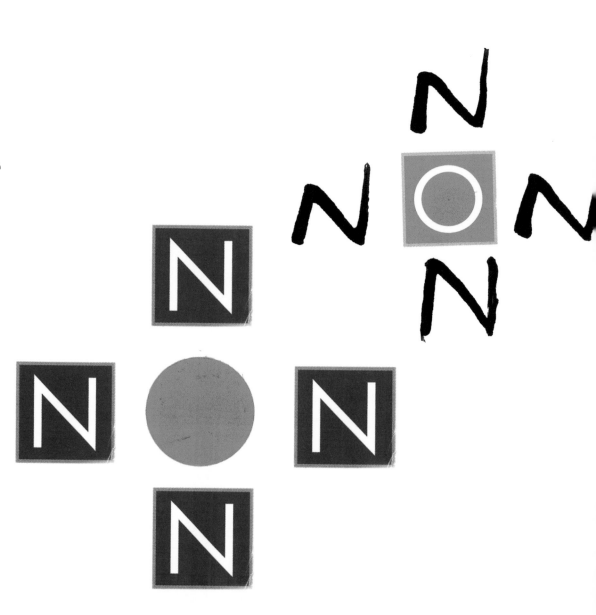

NO Poetry.

Write a poem around the word "No."

No sun—no moon!
No morn—no noon!
No dawn—no dusk—no proper time of day—
No sky—no earthly view—
No distance looking blue—
No road—no street—no "t'other side this way"—
No end to any Row—
No indications where the Crescents go—
No top to any steeple—
No recognitions of familiar people—
No courtesies for showing 'em—
No knowing 'em!
No traveling at all—no locomotion—
No inkling of the way—no notion—
"No go" by land or ocean—
No mail—no post—
No news from any foreign coast—
No Park, no Ring, no afternoon gentility—
No company—no nobility—
No warmth, no cheerfulness, no healthful ease,
No comfortable feel in any member—
No shade, no shine, no butterflies, no bees,
No fruits, no flowers, no leaves, no birds—
November!

—Thomas Hood,
"NO!"

Day 237

I write entirely to find out what I'm thinking, what
I'm looking at, what I see and what it means.
—Joan Didion

F ind some excerpts of poems that
mention the words "see" or "watch" or
"look" and put them in your anthology.
Now read them out loud, one after the
other . . .

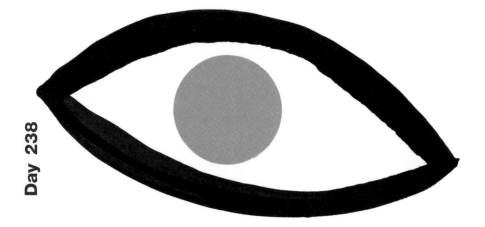

The illusion of art is to make one believe that great literature is very close to life, but exactly the opposite is true. Life is amorphous, literature is formal.
—Françoise Sagan

Write a poem using opposites. For example: word/silence; full/empty; high/low; staying/leaving . . .

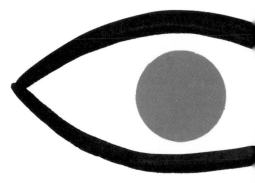

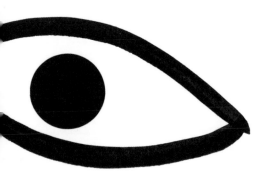

Logical argument is what destroys poetry because poetry is beyond logic.
—Robert Graves

Capitalizing poetry

Capitalizing (or not capitalizing) can be used as a form of expression in poetry. Look through your anthology for poems in which each beginning word in the line is capitalized. What are some of the advantages of capitalization? Experiment with capitalization in your own poetry.

You love the roses—so do I. I wish
The sky would rain down roses, as they rain
From off the shaken bush. Why will it not?
Then all the valley would be pink and white
And soft to tread on. They would fall as light
As feathers, smelling sweet; and it would be
Like sleeping and like waking, all at once!
                    —George Eliot, "Roses"

The poet e. e. cummings never uses capitalization in his poems; in fact, he doesn't capitalize his own name! How does the following excerpt from the poem "i carry your heart with me" benefit from not being capitalized? Does it affect the way you read it?

i carry your heart with me(i carry it in
my heart)i am never without it

Day 241

If you think you can grasp me, think again.
—Adrienne Rich

raw wood
carved wood
stocks of wood
sawed wood
sculpted wood
split wood
gnawed, distorted, uneven wood
broken wood
inflow of wood
curled wood
bitter wood
dry wood

dry rough half-sawn fully splintered sawn through
dry rough split through then partially split
dry rough leveled
[. . .]

—Jean-Marie Gleize

Take some soil in your hands and look at it, knead it, feel it. Now find the words to describe it, imitating the style of Jean-Marie Gleize.

Poetry, O danger of words adrift.
—Louis Aragon

Write a poem that describes, and is shaped like, the following:

a tree
a fish
a star
the sun

One must abolish the adjective to allow the naked
noun to preserve its essential color.
—Filippo Tommaso Marinetti

Write an entirely adjective-free poem.

Poetry is not always words.
—Audrey Foris

Day 245

Take a look at the following:

```
      ‾
     ∪∪
   ‾ ‾ ‾
  ∪∪∪∪
  ∪∪∪∪
   ‾ ‾ ‾
  ∪∪∪∪
  ∪∪∪∪
   ‾ ‾ ‾
     ∪∪
     ‾
```

What do you think this is? A musical score? Morse code? It's a poem by Christian Morgenstern entitled "The Fish's Night Song" (look at it from the side, from top to bottom. Do you see the rough outline of a fish? And the shapes of a fish opening and closing its mouth?) Now create your own poem using symbols, not words.

Manipulating a text

Here is the first stanza of "The Albatross" by Charles Baudelaire:

> Often, for fun, the men of a crew
> Trap albatrosses, those vast sea-birds
> Who lazily pursue the vessel
> Sliding across the deep, salty waters

Replace as many words as you can with a synonym. You could end up with something like this:

> Sometimes, for entertainment, sailors
> Snare albatrosses, of the waters deep
> Indolently following the path of the ship
> As it glides its way across the bitter, heavy gulfs.

Now do the same with the poem's second stanza:

> No sooner have they laid them on the deck
> That these kingly beasts of the sky, clumsy and ashamed,
> Piteously drop their great white wings
> Which trail beside them like useless oars.

Note: Don't attempt a rigorous overhaul of the original wording. This exercise is about gaining more insight into the poem, and strengthening our understanding of it.

A poet can survive everything but a misprint.
—Oscar Wilde

Do yesterday's exercise on one of your OWN poems. Yes, it might be painful . . .

Let the great world spin forever down the ringing grooves
of change.
—Alfred, Lord Tennyson

Playing with antonyms:
Today's new rule: replace every "complete" word
(noun, verb, adjective, or adverb) in the poem "The
Albatross" with its opposite. So "never" replaces
"often," "ewe" replaces "albatross," and "mammal"
replaces "bird," and so on. For example:

> Never, to bore themselves, female officers
> Set free ewes, those little land mammals,
> That energetically flee the train
> As it thunders over the mountaintop.

Using this rule, transform the second stanza of
"The Albatross."

Everywhere I go I find that a poet has been there
before me.
—Sigmund Freud

In today's exercise, you will complete a famous line of poetry using your own words. First, choose a poem and copy its first line into your anthology. Now cross out the second half of the line, leaving only the first half. Invent a new second half. Here is an example, from a line by French poet Alphonse de Lamartine:

O time, halt your flight, and you, propitious hours!

O time, halt your flight! Or else I'll call the police!
O time, halt your flight! It's time for a coffee break!
O time, halt your flight, all the passengers are not yet on board.

What will they say about my poetry / who never
touched my blood?
—Pablo Neruda

Rhetorical question:
A question to which no answer is expected,
and which is posed only for the sake of effect
or emphasis. It's actually not a real question,
but simply a way of making a point. Here
are some examples:

How many times do I have to tell you?
Where does the time go?
Are you crazy?

Rhetorical questions are often used
in poetry. Find some examples and copy
them into your anthology.

Day 250

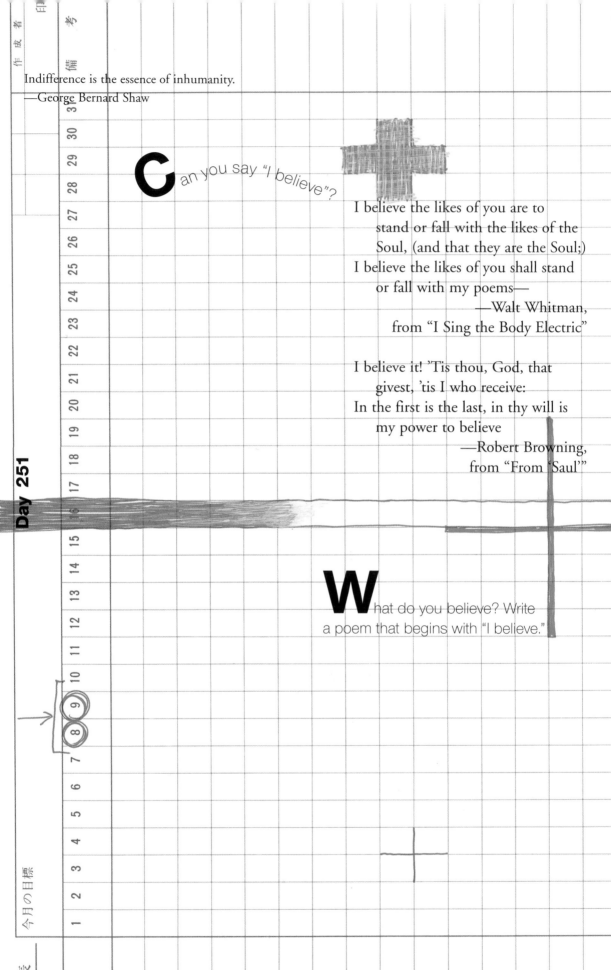

Indifference is the essence of inhumanity.
—George Bernard Shaw

Day 251

Can you say "I believe"?

I believe the likes of you are to
    stand or fall with the likes of the
    Soul, (and that they are the Soul;)
I believe the likes of you shall stand
    or fall with my poems—
           —Walt Whitman,
      from "I Sing the Body Electric"

I believe it! 'Tis thou, God, that
    givest, 'tis I who receive:
In the first is the last, in thy will is
    my power to believe
          —Robert Browning,
      from "From 'Saul'"

What do you believe? Write
a poem that begins with "I believe."

Whether you're a believer or not, write a prayer.

Oh, give us pleasure in the flowers to-day;
And give us not to think so far away
As the uncertain harvest; keep us here
All simply in the springing of the year.

Oh, give us pleasure in the orchard white,
Like nothing else by day, like ghosts by night;
And make us happy in the happy bees,
The swarm dilating round the perfect trees.

And make us happy in the darting bird
That suddenly above the bees is heard,
The meteor that thrusts in with needle bill,
And off a blossom in mid air stands still.

For this is love and nothing else is love,
The which it is reserved for God above
To sanctify to what far ends He will,
But which it only needs that we fulfil.
                    —Robert Frost,
                "A Prayer in Spring"

Day 252

. . . life is not a paragraph, and death i think is no
parenthesis . . .
—e. e. cummings

Gather some poems on the
subject of death and add them to
your anthology.

Because I could not stop for Death,
He kindly stopped for me;
The carriage held but just ourselves
And Immortality.

—Emily Dickinson,
from "Because I could not stop for Death"

Death, I say, my heart is bowed
Unto thine . . .
—Edna St. Vincent Millay

Write a poem about death.

Do not go gentle into that good night,
Old age should burn and rave at close of day
—Dylan Thomas,
from "Do Not Go Gentle into That Good Night"

Several excuses are always less convincing than one.
—Aldous Huxley

Excuses, excuses!

I meant to do my work today,
But a brown bird sang in the apple tree,
—Richard Le Gallienne,
"I Meant to Do My Work"

Now write your own "excuse"
poem, on why you couldn't finish
your homework.

**R**ead the following poem:

> What the hammer? what the chain?
> In what furnace was thy brain?
> What the anvil? what dread grasp
> Dare its deadly terrors clasp?
>
> —William Blake,
> from "The Tyger"

Rewrite, substituting "what" with any other word.
Then create your own poem in the same style.

Day 256

A day may sink or save a realm.
—Alfred, Lord Tennyson

Look for a poem describing the days of the week (or a single day of the week) and copy it into your anthology.

The week had gloomily begun
For Willie Weeks, a poor man's
    SUN.

He was beset with bill and dun,
And he had very little
    MON.

"This cash," said he, "won't pay my dues,
I've nothing here but ones and
    TUES."

                —Carolyn Wells,
           from "A Penitential Week"

Tomorrow, and tomorrow, and tomorrow,
Creeps in this petty pace from day to day…
—William Shakespeare

January brings the snow,
Makes our feet and fingers glow.

February brings the rain,
Thaws the frozen lake again.

March brings breezes loud and shrill,
Stirs the dancing daffodil.

—Sara Coleridge,
from "The Months"

Write a poem that incorporates words and phrases denoting time ("yesterday," "today," "tomorrow," "before," "in the past," "now," "later," "soon") or the months of the year.

アピカ 中性紙使用 ゲン−112 20×20

For everything that's lovely is
But a brief, dreamy kind delight.
—William Butler Yeats

Poem using alliteration

Alliteration is the repetition of the same letter or sounds in words that are close together. Here are some examples from poetry:

I have stood still and stopped the sound of feet . . .
—Robert Frost,
from "Acquainted with the Night"

An old, mad, blind, despised, and dying king,—
Princes, the dregs of their dull race
—Percy Bysshe Shelley,
from "Sonnet: England in 1819"

So your chimneys I sweep and in soot I sleep . . .
—William Blake,
from "The Chimney Sweeper"

Find some other examples of alliteration in poetry and copy them into your anthology.

We have all some experience of a feeling, that comes
over us occasionally, of what we are saying and doing
having been said and done before, in a remote time . . .
—Charles Dickens

Déjà-vu

Déjà-vu literally means "already seen";
it is a feeling of already having experienced
or seen something before. Look at this
poetic example:

I have been here before,
But when or how I cannot tell:
I know the grass beyond the door,
The sweet keen smell,
The sighing sound, the lights around the shore.
                            —Dante Gabriel Rossetti,
                                from "Sudden Light"

Now write (poetically, of course)
about your own experience of déjà-vu.

Letters are among the most significant memorial a person can leave
behind them.
—Johann Wolfgang von Goethe

Letter-poem

Compose a poem written in the
style of a letter (or an e-mail!)

Dear Danny, I'm taking the pen in my hand,
To tell you we're just out of sight of the land,
In the grand Allen liner I'm sailing in style,
But I'm sailing away from the Emerald Isle.
And a long sort of sigh seemed to come from us all
When the waves hit the last bit of auld Donegal,
Ah, it's well to be you that is taking your tay,
Where' they're cutting the corn in Creeslough today.

There's a woman on board who knows Katie by sight,
And we talked of auld times 'til they put out the light.
I'm to meet the good woman tomorrow on deck,
And we'll talk about Katie from here to Quebec,
I know I'm no match for her, no not the least
With her house and two cows, and her brother a priest.
But the woman declares Katie's heart's on the say,
While mine's with the reaper's in Creeslough today.

Ah, goodbye to you Danny, no more's to be said,
And I think the salt water's got into my head,
For it drips from my eyes when I call to my mind
The friends and the colleagues I'm leaving behind.
But still she might wait. When I bade her goodbye
There was just the least trace of a tear in her eye,
And a brake in her voice when she said, "You might stay,
But, please God you'll return to auld Creeslough, some day.

—Percy French,
"The Emigrant's Letter"

Sometimes poetry is used as a protest, or to defend an idea. Compose a passionate, poetic appeal on a subject that matters to you.

> Yes, injured Woman! rise, assert thy right!
> Woman! too long degraded, scorned, opprest;
> O born to rule in partial Law's despite,
> Resume thy native empire o'er the breast!
>
> Go forth arrayed in panoply divine;
> That angel pureness which admits no stain;
> Go, bid proud Man his boasted rule resign,
> And kiss the golden sceptre of thy reign.
> —Anna Letitia Barbauld,
> from "The Rights of Women"

Day 262

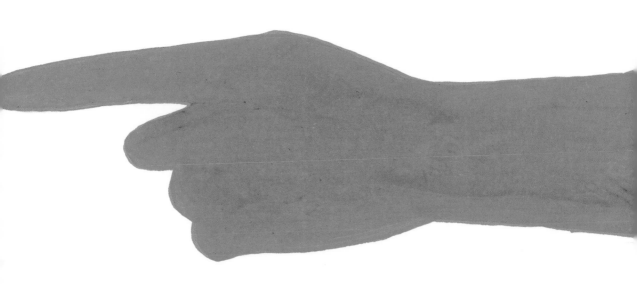

A photograph is usually looked at—seldom looked into.
—Ansel Adams

Choose a photograph and describe what you see.

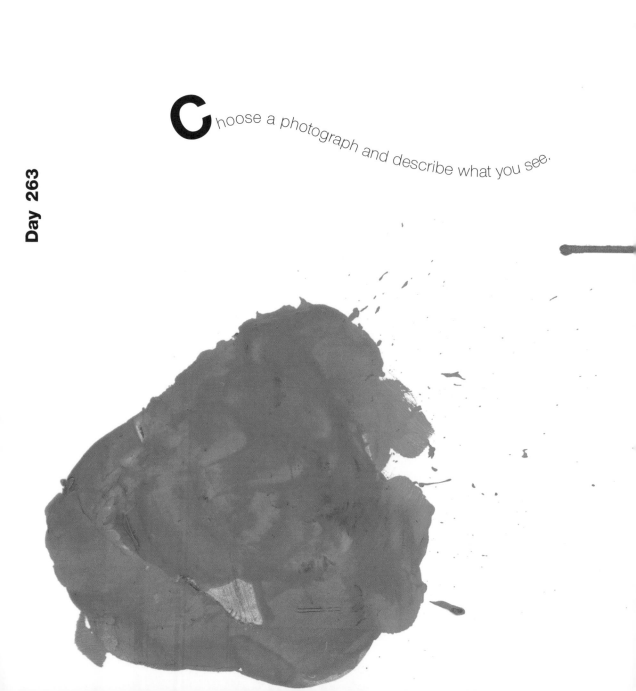

Painting is poetry that is seen rather than felt, and
poetry is painting that is felt rather than seen.
—Leonardo da Vinci

Just as painters have turned to poetry
for inspiration, poets have often been
inspired by paintings. William Carlos
Williams famously contemplated the art
of Brueghel, Allen Ginsberg mused on
Cézanne, and Paul Engle wrote of Titian.

Now it's your turn. Write a poem that
describes, or interprets, a painting of
your choice.

Day 264

Put your ear down close to your soul and listen hard.
—Anne Sexton

What is your mood today? Are you
sad, joyous, nervous,
excited, furious?

Transcribe your mood into words.

Stranger, if you passing meet me and desire to speak to me, why should you not speak to me? And why should I not speak to you?
—Walt Whitman

Think of a poet (either dead or alive) that particularly inspires you. Now make a list of questions you would like to ask him or her.

Man can learn nothing except by going from the
known to the unknown.
—Claude Bernard

A day of discovery.
Are there some poets whose work is
still unfamiliar to you, but which you
would like to learn more about? Today,
choose the work of three "undiscovered"
poets and copy one (or more) of their
poems into your anthology.

In character, in manner, in style, in all things, the
supreme excellence is simplicity.
—Henry Wadsworth Longfellow

A lesson in simplicity.

Still pond—skipping stone—
ripples in water

In this poem, the poet uses concrete
imagery to capture the spirit of a
moment, communicating much using
only a few, simple words.

Now imitate that style,
substituting "old pond"
with the following:

Mountain stream—
New swimming pool—

Day 268

The art of art, the glory of expression and the sunshine
of the light of letters, is simplicity.
—Walt Whitman

Haiku are a form of Japanese poem, that has a total of three lines. The first line usually contains five syllables, the second line seven, and third five syllables again.

Snow falls in deep night
a soft blanket on the ground
The round moon—silence

Compose your own haiku (or two or three . . .)

Narrative poems are poems that tell a story. They can take the form of verse or prose. Like a short story, narrative poems have characters and plots. Find some examples of narrative poetry and put them in your anthology. One of the most famous narrative poems is Samuel Taylor Coleridge's "The Rime of the Ancient Mariner," which begins like this:

It is an ancient Mariner,
And he stoppeth one of three.
"By thy long beard and glittering eye,
Now wherefore stopp'st thou me?

The Bridegroom's doors are opened wide,
And I am next of kin;
The guests are met, the feast is set:
May'st hear the merry din."

There is no agony like bearing an untold story inside of you.
—Maya Angelou

Write your own narrative poem, in prose or in verse. To help you, here are the beginning lines of some poems:

It was many and many a year ago . . .
            —Edgar Allan Poe,
                from "Annabel Lee"

I awoke happy . . .
            —William Carlos
                    Williams,
            from "The Revelation"

I met a traveller from an antique land . . .
            —Percy Bysshe Shelley,
                from "Ozymandias"

A string-along poem

In today's poem, a word from the
previous line is used as a springboard
for the next line, such as this popular
nursery rhyme:

A man of words and not of deeds,
Is like a garden full of weeds;
And when the weeds begin to grow,
It's like a garden full of snow;
And when the snow begins to fall,
It's like a bird upon the wall;
And when the bird away does fly,
It's like an eagle in the sky;
And when the sky begins to roar,
It's like a lion at the door […]

Try writing a poem using the same style.

A Poem should be palpable and mute
As a globed fruit.
—Archibald MacLeish

Still-life poetry.
In painting, a still-life depicts
inanimate objects, either alone or
grouped together. (Think of some
Impressionist paintings of flower
arrangements or fruit bowls.) Why
not try a still-life poem, such as the
one below?

So snug, so compact, so wise are we!
Under the kitchen-table leg
My knee is pressing against his knee.
Our shutters are shut, the fire is low,
The tap is dripping peacefully;
The saucepan shadows on the wall
Are black and round and plain to see.
—Katherine Mansfield,
from "Camomile Tea"

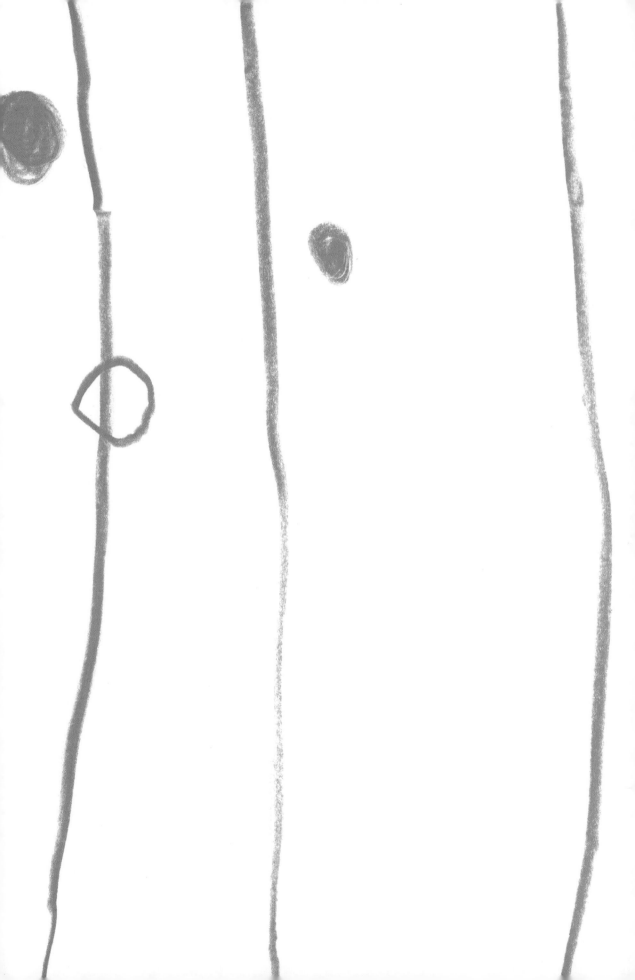

T

E

Y

X

Z

W

K

The things we have to learn before we can do them, we
learn by doing them.
—Aristotle

Choose two words out of the
dictionary that are unfamiliar to you.
Without looking at their definition,
use them to write today's poem.

Confronted with the question "Why do you write?"
the Poet's answer is always the shortest: "To live better."
—Saint-John Perse

Ask yourself this question yet again. You may find that you have new answers.

The voyage of discovery is not in seeking new
landscapes but in having new eyes.
—Marcel Proust

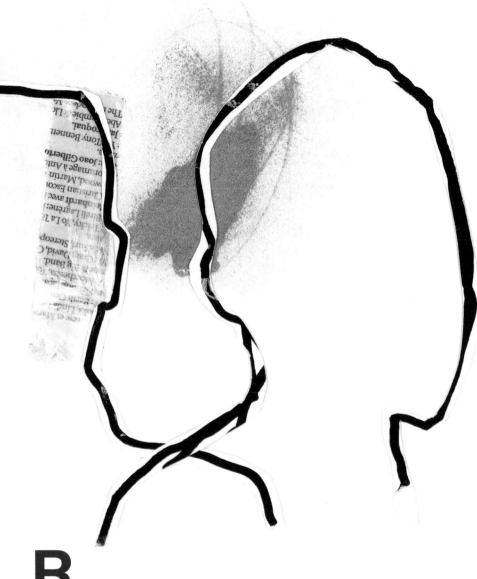

Day 276

Read the newspaper and write a
poem on a news item of your choice.

Poetry—our poetry—reads like a newspaper. The
newspaper of a world yet to come.
—Louis Aragon

Find a poem for your anthology that
fits this definition of poetry.

A mathematical poem? That's today's challenge.

Day 278

Arithmetic is where numbers fly like pigeons in and out of your head.
Arithmetic tells you how many you lose or win if you know how
  many you had before you lost or won.

—Carl Sandburg,
from "Arithmetic"

The world is mud-luscious and puddle-wonderful.
—e. e. cummings

Today, go outside and get your hands dirty! Look underneath a rock, examine the roots of a tree, or dig through some soil and write about whatever you find lurking there.

To see a world in a grain of sand
And a heaven in a wild flower,
Hold infinity in the palm of your hand
And eternity in an hour.

—William Blake,
from "Auguries of Innocence"

Everything one invents is true, you may be perfectly
sure of that. Poetry is as precise as geometry.
—Gustave Flaubert

65

Day 280

Transform a geometry problem, a
grammar rule, or a biology lesson into
poetry.

Two roads diverged in a wood, and I—
I took the one less traveled by,
And that has made all the difference.
—Robert Frost

A "direction-poem"

Start by reading this poem by
Henry Wadsworth Longfellow:

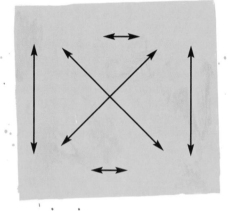

By the shore of Gitchie Gumee,
By the shining Big-Sea-Water,
At the doorway of his wigwam,
In the pleasant Summer morning,
Hiawatha stood and waited.
All the air was full of freshness,
All the earth was bright and joyous,
And before him through the sunshine,
Westward toward the neighboring forest
Passed in golden swarms the Ahmo,
Passed the bees, the honey-makers,
Burning, singing in the sunshine.
Bright above him shown the heavens,
Level spread the lake before him; [. . .]
       —Henry Wadsworth Longfellow,
         from "Song of Hiawatha"

Now write a poem for your modern
environment, giving directions to either
your school, local supermarket, post
office, or your best friend's house. Think
about the landmarks, signposts and
other distinguishing features that would
help guide a person there . . .

Poetry is above all a concentration of the power of
language, which is the power of our ultimate
relationship to everything in the universe.
—Adrienne Rich

In translations of poetry, words can be interpreted in a number of different ways. Here, for example, is "The Emperor Tenchi" in the original Japanese, from *Hyakunin-isshu* (A Hundred Verses from Old Japan) and two translations:

Tenchi Tennō

Aki no ta no
Kari ho no iho no
Toma wo arami
Waga koromode wa
Tsuyu ni nure-tsutsu.

William N. Porter proposed this translation:

Out in the fields this autumn day
They're busy reaping grain;
I sought for shelter 'neath this roof,
But fear I sought in vain—
My sleeve is wet with rain.

Clay McCauley proposed this translation:

Coarse the rush-mat roof
Sheltering the harvest-hut
Of the autumn rice-field;—
And my sleeves are growing wet
With the moisture dripping through.

The poem is about the Emperor Tenchi reflecting on his poor subjects' hard lot in life. Compare the two translations and suggest a third one, in haiku form or free verse.

Day 282

Poetry is a way of taking life by the throat.
—Robert Frost

Personification

A figure of speech that attributes human characteristics or qualities to objects or nonhumans. It is used widely in both poetry and prose. Look at the following example:

The Train
I like to see it lap the miles,
And lick the valleys up,
And stop to feed itself at tanks;
And then, prodigious, step
Around a pile of mountains [. . .]

—Emily Dickinson,
from "The Train"

Find some other classic examples of personification and put them in your anthology.

The earth laughs in flowers.
—e. e. cummings

Can you guess? Today, write your OWN poem using personification.

The sun illuminates only the eye of the man, but
shines into the eye and the heart of the child.
—Ralph Waldo Emerson

There was a crooked man, and he went a crooked mile,
And found a crooked sixpence against a crooked stile,
He bought a crooked cat, which caught a crooked mouse,
And they all lived together in a little crooked house.

An old Mother Goose rhyme

Choose several poems for a young child.

May the child's voice inside you never grow silent.
—Louis-René Desforêts

Write a poem for the child you once were.

Writing is a way of speaking without being interrupted.
—Jules Renard

Writing in flux

Choose any word or a fragment of a sentence from a collection of poems. Copy it, and immediately prolong it, by adding the first words or thoughts that pop into your head. Don't stop! Continue writing this way, without lifting your hand, without breathing, for as long as you can.

Put it aside until tomorrow.

Take the text you wrote yesterday. Without altering or editing it in any way, remove a passage and copy it here. Notice how, in a different context, it takes on a completely new meaning.

Day 288

He who has no poetry in himself will find poetry in nothing.
—Joseph Joubert

Reread your original text from a couple days ago. This time, feel free to rewrite or delete various passages. Playing with various poetic tools (the introduction of white space, repetition, forms of punctuation, capitalization, etc.), present your text as a complete work of poetry.

Writing and rewriting are a constant search for what it
is one is saying.
—John Updike

Apply yesterday's technique to a handful of your poems. Take some time to reread them, and edit or reconfigure any that needs it. Use any poetic techniques at your disposal to finesse your poetry.

Not deep the poet sees, but wide.
—Matthew Arnold

What if you made a tour of the world in 80 poems?

That's certainly a way of enriching your anthology. Start by selecting a poem from every continent.

The poet remembers the future.
—Jean Cocteau

Imagine a poem from the 22nd century, a science-fiction poem, essentially.

Day 292

. . . silent, gazing, pondering the themes thou lovest best.
Night, sleep, and the stars.
—Walt Whitman

Write in the early morning, *after a night spent reading poetry.*

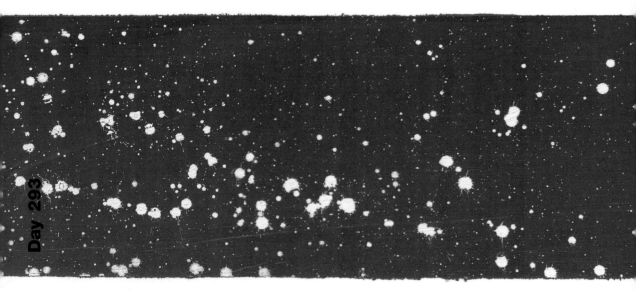

Day 293

Weary with toil, I haste me to my bed
The dear repose for limbs with travel tired;
But then begins a journey in my head
To work my mind, when body's work's expir'd:
For then my thoughts—from far where I abide—
Intend a zealous pilgrimage to thee,
And keep my drooping eyelids open wide,
Looking on darkness which the blind do see:
Save that my soul's imaginary sight
Presents thy shadow to my sightless view,
Which, like a jewel hung in ghastly night,
Makes black night beauteous and her old face new.
　　Lo! thus, by day my limbs, by night my mind,
　　For thee, and for myself no quiet find.
　　　　　　　　　　　—William Shakespeare,
　　　　　　　　　　　　"Sonnet 27"

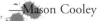

Parodies

Many poets have written parodies (either respectful or mocking) of famous poems.

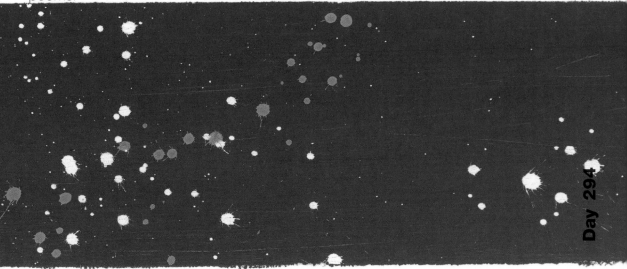

Day 294

Read "My Heart Leaps Up" by William Wordsworth out loud:

> My heart leaps up when I behold
> A rainbow in the sky.
> So was it when my life began;
> So is it now I am a man;
> So be it when I grow old,
> Or let me die!
> The Child is father of the Man;
> And I could wish my days to be
> Bound each to each by natural piety.

Now read this parody, "The Child Is Father to the Man," by Gerard Manley Hopkins:

> "The child is father to the man."
> How can he be? The words are wild.
> Suck any sense from that who can:
> "The child is father to the man."
> No; what the poet did write ran,
> "The man is father to the child."
> "The child is father to the man!"
> How can he be? The words are wild.

Analyze a poem (or a line of a poem) that you either particularly enjoy or dislike, or question, and write your own version of it based on the original.

All our words are but crumbs that fall down from the
feast of the mind.
—Kahlil Gibran

Find some poems whose shape or
layout is one of the defining elements of
its intended poetic effect.

Learn more about visual poetry. You
can start by visiting the following website:
www.costis.org

Day 296

The pages are still blank, but there is a miraculous feeling of the words being there, written in invisible ink and clamoring to become visible.
—Vladimir Nabokov

I AM HERE

Same words, different meaning.
Propose another layout, which would give an entirely new meaning to these words.

I am here

Can you suggest a layout for this line from "13 Ways of Looking at a Blackbird" by Wallace Stevens that would give it more impact, more poetic effect?

Among twenty snowy mountains, the only moving thing was the eye of the blackbird.

Submit several propositions.

Day 298

Words are but the vague shadows of the volumes we mean. Little audible links, they are, chaining together great inaudible feelings and purposes.
—Theodore Dreiser

Choose one of your poems and write it in the form of a poster.

Reality only reveals itself when it is illuminated by a
ray of poetry.
—Georges Braque

Read Apollinaire's poem "Singer" again.

and the sole string of the sea trumpets

What kind of effect does this poem
have when it is written this way?
Does it appeal more to your sense of
sight or hearing now? Would it strike you
differently if it were broken up into lines?
Now write your own single-line poem in
the same style.

Day 300

To see the Summer Sky
Is Poetry, though never in a Book it lie—
True Poems flee.
—Emily Dickinson

Day 301

Play with the layout of several of your own poems.

Poems in motion: Instead of formatting one of your poems on a single page, why not copy it into a notebook of eight or sixteen pages?

Day 302

Images, which are the life of poetry, cannot be raised
in any perfection but by introducing particular objects.
—Henry Home, Lord Kames

A voluminous poem: Format your poem in the shape of a mobile, or a parallelogram.

Painting is silent poetry, and poetry is painting with
the gift of speech.
—Simonides

A number of painters have
illustrated poems.
Find some examples.

Day 304

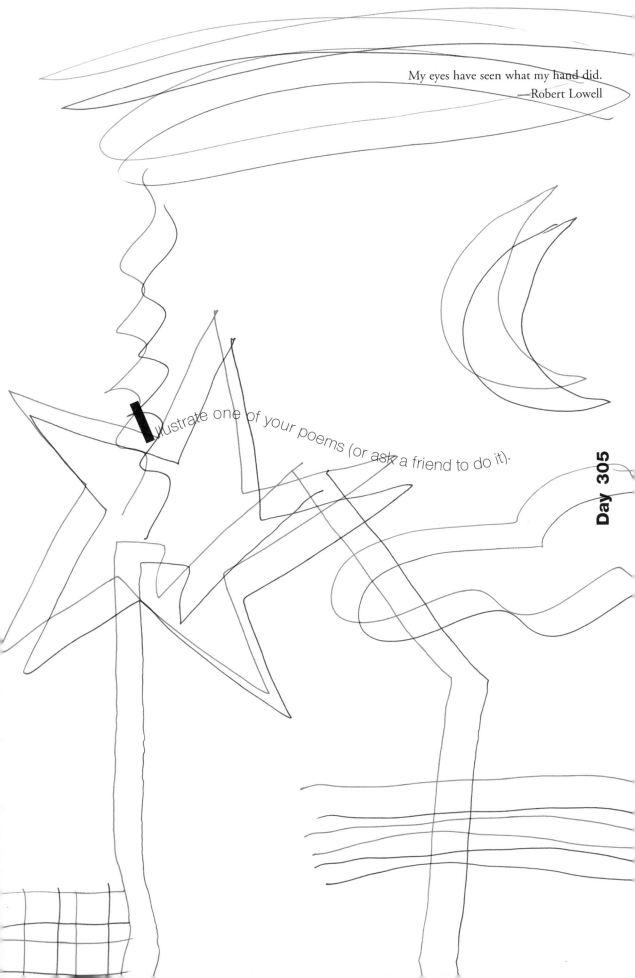

My eyes have seen what my hand did.
—Robert Lowell

Illustrate one of your poems (or ask a friend to do it).

Day 305

Everything you can imagine is real.
—Pablo Picasso

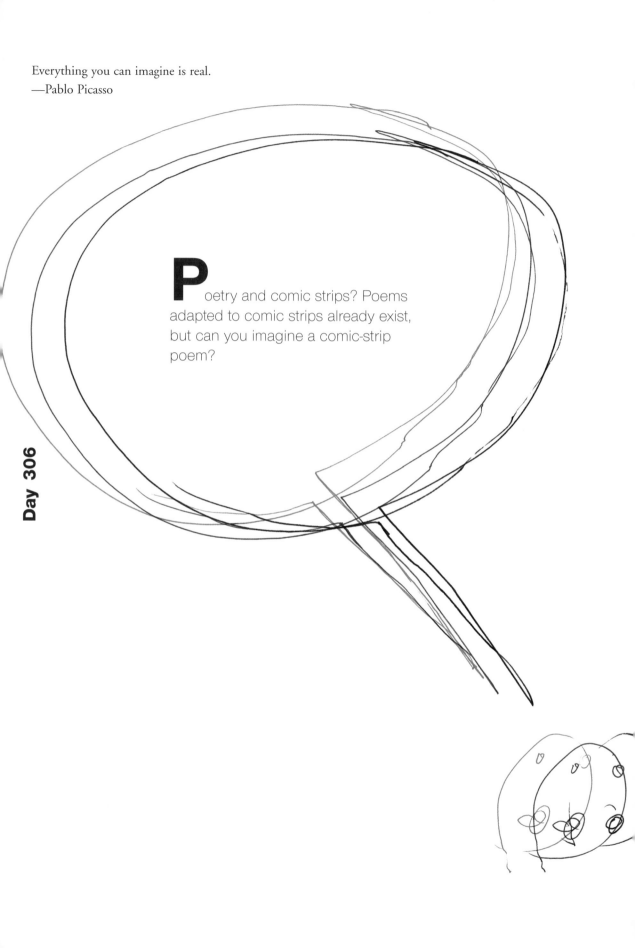

Poetry and comic strips? Poems adapted to comic strips already exist, but can you imagine a comic-strip poem?

It is requisite for the relaxation of the mind that we make
use, from time to time, of playful deeds and jokes.
—St. Thomas Aquinas

Modify a traditional game (such
as dominoes or cards) to make a game-
poem.

Day 307

Poetry is that art which selects and arranges the symbols of thought in such a manner as to excite the imagination the most powerfully and delightfully.
—William Cullen Bryant

Day 1

The next nine days will be devoted to writing your longest poem yet. Are you ready for the adventure? To begin, here are several fragments to inspire you. Choose one of them and expand on it, develop a theme. Look for movement and continuity. Don't get bogged down by details. Write "lengthily."

Nothing had changed yet

snow snow snow ah white

sometimes I write in prose

my prayer this is how my prayer begins

Sleep
Sleep
Sleep
Sleep
You

I say NO to extortionists, prosecutors, professors, computers

A piece of advice: When you get stuck, repeat a phrase you already wrote. Repetition can help jump-start your writing.

Writing is both mask and unveiling.
—E. B. White

Day 2

Read what you wrote yesterday out loud. Now turn the page. Copy the last sentence from the day before and continue writing . . .

Fill your paper with the breathings of your heart.
—William Wordsworth

Day 3

Read out loud what you wrote yesterday, but this time read it backwards, starting with the last line. Ask yourself this question: what is the central point that your text revolves around—is it a word, an idea, a shape?

Day 4

Without rereading what you have already
written, take your text from yesterday and
keep writing, several times
               throughout the day.
Remember to not look back.

There are three things, after all, that a poem must reach: the eye, the ear, and what we may call the heart or the mind. It is most important of all to reach the heart of the reader.
—Robert Frost

Day 5

Reread your entire poem.
Today you're going to intervene and take it in a new direction. Introduce a new theme, or a new rhythm. If you wish, you can incorporate one of the following fragments:

Day 312

above the clouds

who's there?

and again and again and again

One speaks
One lives

Maybe
Just maybe

ah ah ah ah ah ah

Poetry is like a bird, it ignores all frontiers.
—Yevgeny Yevtushenko

Day 313

Day 6

Take the first line of your poem. Copy it down on another sheet of paper and start again. Write anew, paying no attention to what you have already written.

Poets should ignore most criticism and get on with making poetry.
—Anne Stevenson

Day 7

On the seventh day, as you know, we rest. Nevertheless, reread your text, your longest poem yet. Choose one of the following methods to rework it: **erase** some isolated words (an adjective here, a verb there); **omit** the obvious; introduce **silence** by creating white space, either by breaking up lines, or even skipping lines; insert **rhythm** by repeating certain words, fragments, lines or entire passages.

In poetry, you must love the words, the ideas and the images and rhythms with all your capacity to love at all.
—Wallace Stevens

Day 8

Copy your poem on a new sheet of paper.

The end of writing is to instruct; the end of poetry is
to instruct by pleasing.
—Samuel Johnson

Day 9

W ho will you dedicate your poem to?

Day 316

A poem is energy transferred from where the poet got it,
by way of the poem itself, all the way over to the reader.
—Charles Olson

Day 317

Among all the poems in your anthology, which would you have liked dedicated to you?

And I who considered myself a poet, I couldn't find the words to call the sun.
—René Daumal

A nd you, can you "find the words to call the sun"? Or rain?

Day 318

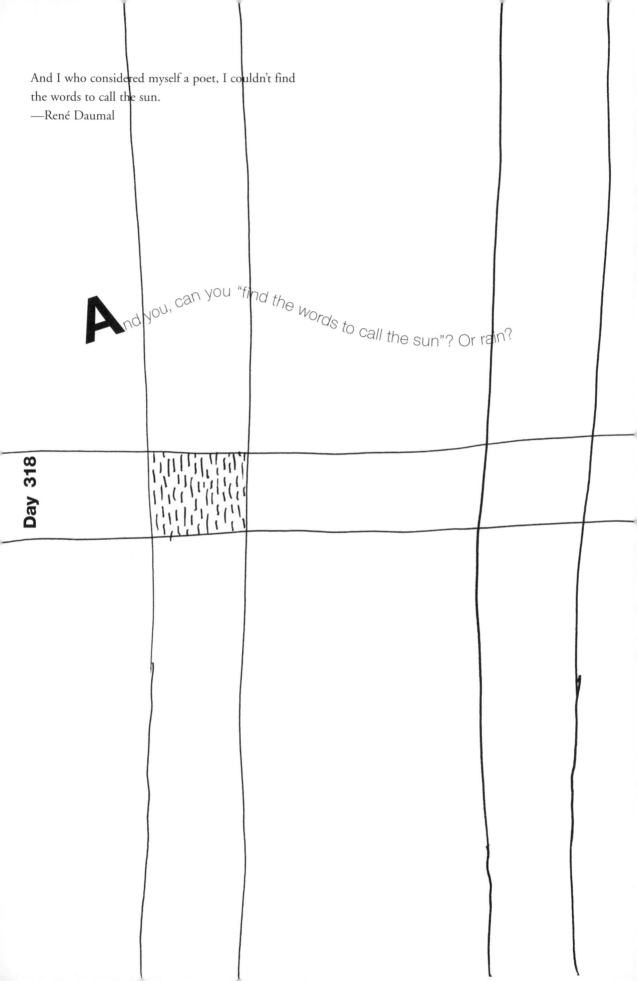

Poetry: Imaginary gardens with real toads in them.
—Marianne Moore

Day 319

"Imaginary gardens with real toads": What else is in poetry's imaginary garden?

Poetry is concerned with using with abusing, with
losing with wanting, with denying with avoiding with
adoring with replacing the noun . . .
—Gertrude Stein

"Undo" one of your poems (a short one). Write each word of the poem on a separate strip of paper. Using these words, compose an entirely new poem.

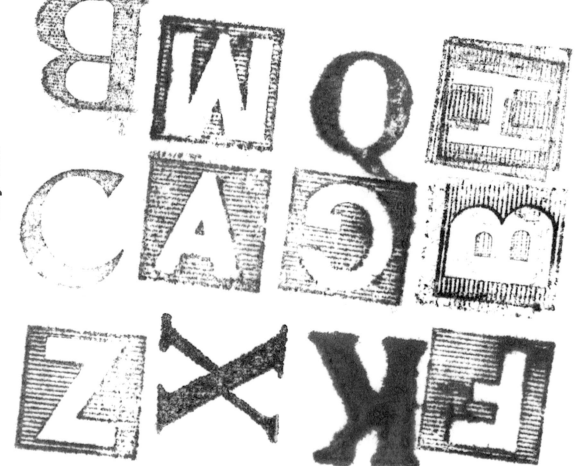

What are some of the poetic tools you use most often? Rhyme? Repetition? Metaphors? Why?

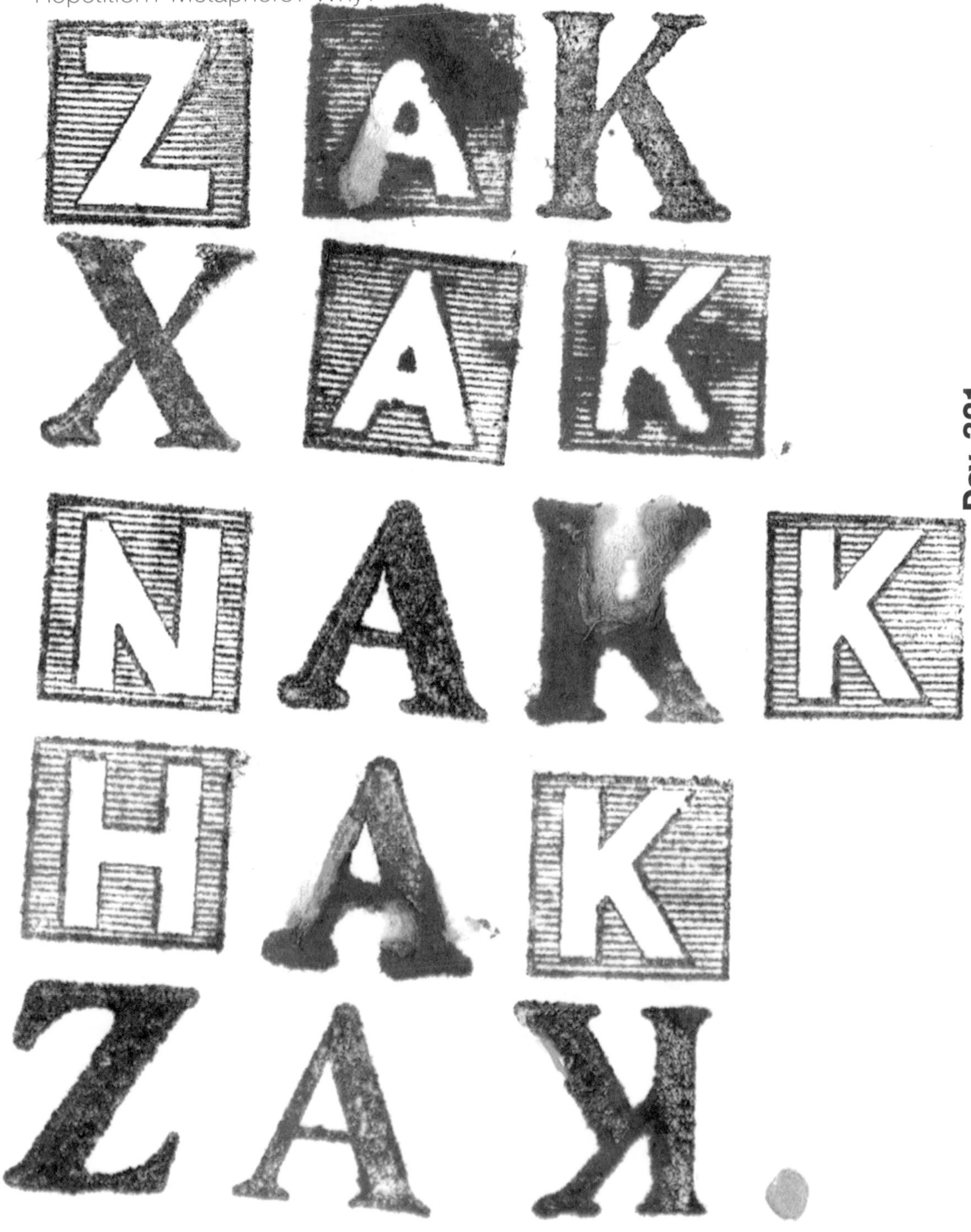

ZAK
XAK AK
NAK K
HAK
ZAK.

Day 321

Rhyme, that enslaved queen, that supreme charm of
our poetry, that creator of our meter.
—Victor Hugo

Today, take some time
to work on rhyme . . .

A couplet, two lines of verse joined by rhyme, is
the simplest rhyming verse. Read the following
couplet from Alexander Pope's "An Essay on
Criticism" out loud:

True wit is nature to advantage dressed,
What oft was thought, but ne'er so well expressed.

Look for rhyming couplets in collections of poems, or in your own anthology.

I thought of rhyme alone,
For rhyme can beat a measure out of trouble
And make the daylight sweet once more . . .
—William Butler Yeats

Why stop at a couplet? Adding a
third rhyming line results in a triplet, such
as in "The Three Voices" by Lewis Carroll:

He trilled a carol fresh and free,
He laughed aloud for very glee:
There came a breeze from off the sea:

It passed athwart the glooming flat—
It fanned his forehead as he sat—
It lightly bore away his hat,

All to the feet of one who stood
Like maid enchanted in a wood,
Frowning as darkly as she could.

Day 323

The chances of rhyme are like the chances of meeting—
In the finding fortuitous, but once found binding.
—Charles Tomlinson

A quatrain is a section of poetry composed of four lines having alternate rhymes. Read this fragment of "With Rue My Heart Is Laden" by A. E. Housman out loud:

With rue my heart is laden
For golden friends I had,
For many a rose-lipt maiden
And many a lightfoot lad.

The rhyming scheme in that stanza is *abab*. But you can also have *abba*, as in this verse by Alfred, Lord Tennyson from "In Memoriam":

Are God and Nature then at strife,
That Nature lends such evil dreams?
So careful of the type she seems,
So careless of the single life

Explore all the various kinds of rhyming quatrains and copy your favorites in your anthology.

Compose another list-poem. For example, a list of your favorite television programs, or your likes and dislikes. This time, however, introduce rhyme.

> There was a naughty boy,
>   A naughty boy was he,
> He would not stop at home,
>   He could not quiet be–
>   He took
>   In his knapsack
>   A book
>   Full of vowels
>   And a shirt
>   With some towels
>   A slight cap
>   For night-cap,
>   A hair-brush,
>   Comb ditto,
>   New stockings,
>   For old ones
>   Would split O!
>   —John Keats,
>   from "A Song About Myself"

Another idea: Make a collage of various excerpts of your poems using, of course, rhymes.

Day 325

Poetry consists in a rhyming dictionary and things
seen.
—Gertrude Stein

Day 326

A bit of rhyme:
Write a quatrain that uses the rhyming
scheme *abba*, with each line ending
with the following words:

you
eye
sky
true

Rhyme, the rack of finest wits,
That expresseth but by fits . . .
—Ben Jonson

Read out loud this excerpt of
Edgar Allan Poe's "The Raven," in which
many of the rhymes are internal. Who
said rhymes always had to come at the
end of the line?

Once upon a midnight dreary, while I pondered, weak and weary,
Over many a quaint and curious volume of forgotten lore,
While I nodded, nearly napping, suddenly there came a tapping,
As of someone gently rapping, rapping at my chamber door.
" 'Tis some visitor," I muttered, "tapping at my chamber door;
Only this, and nothing more."

Find some other examples of internal
rhyme in poetry collections (or in your
own poems).

Day 327

I am a poet, but I don't want to be a poet for others.
—Sören Kierkegaard

Do you share this belief? Or do you want to submit your texts for others to read? Ask yourself whom you want to share them with, and how. (For example, think about the number of Internet sites where you might post your poems).

Why not organize a poetry meeting (a reading, informal discussion, or an Internet forum?) For two, ten, or a hundred people . . . .

Day 329

The poet enjoys the incomparable privilege of being
able to be himself and others, as he wishes.
—Charles Baudelaire

Share with others the experience of
writing poetry. Think of an exercise that
was particularly beneficial to you and
have them complete it.

"A poet is a man speaking to men":
But I am then a poet, am I not?
—John Berryman

Do a "poetic interview" on a poet of your choice. Some of the answers to your questions can be excerpts from their poems.

A poet is a combination of an instrument and a
human being in one person, with the former gradually
taking over the latter.
—Joseph Brodsky

Write to a poet, and maybe even send him or her some of your own poems.

A poet's work is to name the unnameable, to point at frauds, to take sides, start arguments, shape the world, and stop it going to sleep.
—Salman Rushdie

Encourage one of your friends to write a poem—maybe even their first poem.

The poem invents his poet.
The reader continues the poem.
The reader invents the poet.
—Alain Bosquet

Day 334

In the morning, read a poem by a contemporary poet. Reread it at noon. In the evening, without rereading it, respond to the poem by composing a poem of your own.

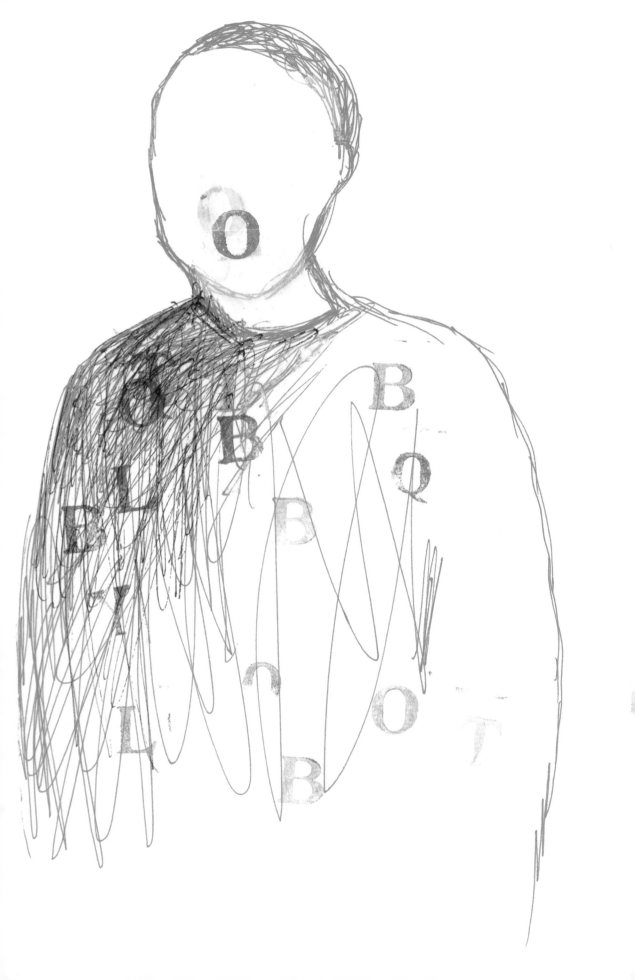

Almost no one likes poems and the world of verse is a
fiction and a falsehood.
—Witold Gombrowicz

What can you say **against** poetry?

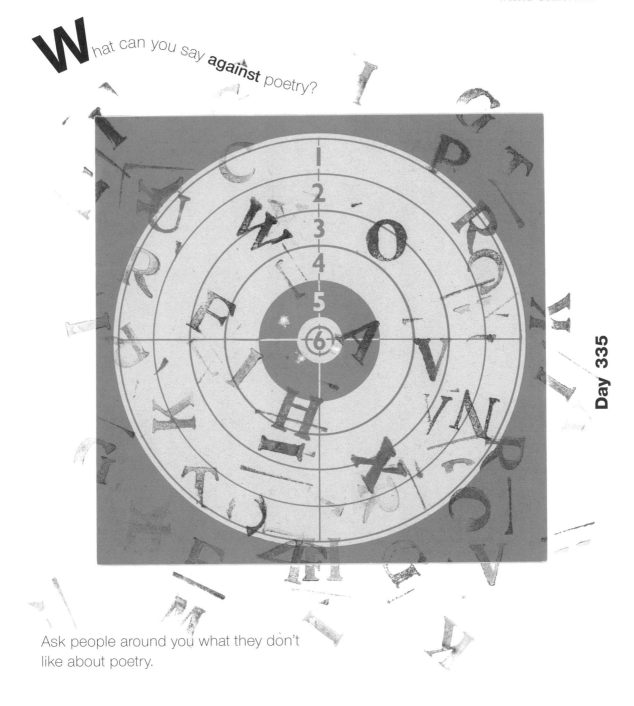

Ask people around you what they don't
like about poetry.

In poetry, it's the excess that wearies; the excess of poetry, poetic words, metaphors, sublimations, finally, the excess of condensation and purification of all antipoetic elements, which results in poems similar to chemical products. How did we arrive at this point?
—Witold Gombrowicz

Write a pamphlet against poetry (maybe using the format of . . . a poem).

Day 336

My father used to say that poetry is only good for geese, birds and the idle rich and you'd be better off learning the civil code.
—Jean-Claude Pirotte

Write a dialogue between several people, some of whom defend poetry and others who critique it. One way of writing it would be to have each person expressing him- or herself in a different style.

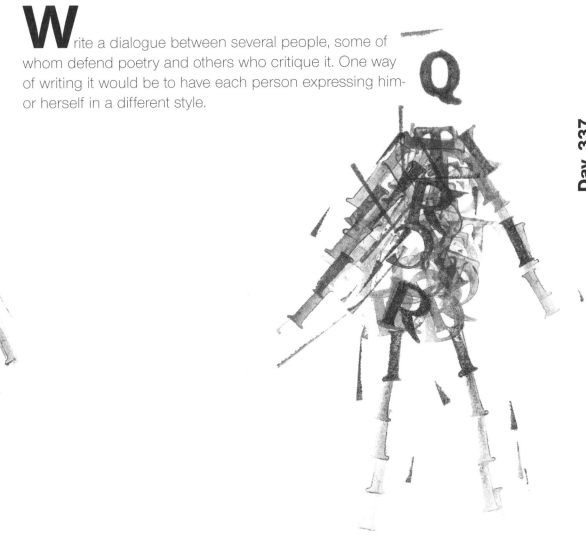

Poetry is a beautiful way of spoiling prose, and the laborious art of exchanging plain sense for harmony.
—Horace Walpole

Here are some other reflections on poetry:

Poetry is in constant rebellion against itself.

—Mahmoud Darwish

The revolt against poetry continues. No more literature!

—Antonin Artaud

Much of our poetry has the very best manners, but no character.

—Henry David Thoreau

Writing poetry is often writing against poetry.

—Christian Prigent

"Writing against poetry": What do you think that means? Can you give some examples of writing "against poetry"?

Poetry is man's rebellion against being what he is.
—James Branch Cabell

Write a "rebellious" poem.

Day 339

The poet must be able to say anything with complete freedom. Try it, my friends, and you'll see that you're not free.
—Robert Desnos

Yes, try.

Try, for example, to talk about something you've never spoken about before. It's OK: no one will read it. Except, of course, YOU.

Day 340

Such is the role of poetry. It unveils, in the strict sense of the word. It lays bare, under a light which shakes off torpor, the surprising things which surround us and which our senses record mechanically.
—Jean Cocteau

Can you "unveil" and "lay bare" a scene or experience during the course of your day? Try to use real, unadorned language. Truly describe what is happening around you.

Day 341

Poetry . . . seeks a hold upon reality, and the closeness
of its approach is the test of its success.
—Babette Deutsch

Write a poem on one of the following
subjects:

a pizza box thrown in the street
a car's engine
the price of gasoline
a video game
makeup remover
pesticides

We define poetry as the unofficial view of being.
—Wallace Stevens

Describe what you understand as the "unofficial" view of being, as opposed to the "official" one.

Day 343

Why is it that the poet tells
So little of the sense of smell?
—Christopher Morley

Day 344

One strength of a poem lies in its ability to appeal to one (or more) of our senses, for example our sense of smell. Can you smell the odors described in this excerpt of "Smells" by Christopher Morley?

These are the odors I love well:

The smell of coffee freshly ground;
Or rich plum pudding, holly crowned;
Or onions fried and deeply browned.

The fragrance of a fumy pipe;
The smell of apples, newly ripe;
And printer's ink on leaden type.

Woods by moonlight in September
Breathe most sweet, and I remember
Many a smoky camp-fire ember.

Camphor, turpentine, and tea,
The balsam of a Christmas tree,
These are whiffs of gramarye . . .
A ship smells best of all to me!

Find some examples of poems that appeal to any of our senses and copy them into your anthology.

Beautiful day?

Write a poem in which it's raining cats and dogs.

Gloomy day?

Write a poem in which the sun radiates downward, bathing everything in light.

All the soarings of my mind begin in my blood.
—Rainer Maria Rilke

Add some disturbing poems to your poetry anthology.

Writing
is digging in the dark.
—Guillevic

Write on this black page.

Day 347

Great poetry is always written by somebody straining
to go beyond what he can do.
—Stephen Spender

Day 348

Surpass, exceed, go further than you think you can . . .

finally

disappeared

there

you

Continue adding words to this image,
writing both inside and outside the frame.

I grew up in this town, my poetry was born between the hill and the river, it took its voice from the rain, and like the timber, it steeped itself in the forests.
—Pablo Neruda

Day 349

I grew up . . . | My poetry was born . . . | It took its voice . . .

And you? Finish these thoughts.

A short poem to the left.
Prose to the right.
—Alain Bosquet

Follow the directions of Alain
Bosquet to the letter:
At the left of the page,
write a "short poem."
And to the right, a text in prose.

A sentence that opens.
A sentence that closes up.
—Alain Bosquet

Day 351

Invent a poem alternating between sentences that open and those that close.

How do poems grow? They grow out of your life.
—Robert Penn Warren

Among all the activities in this journal, pick out the three that you enjoyed the most. Among the three, choose one and do it again today.

That a poem speaks of love or politics, it's all the same.
It's not what it says that makes the difference.
—Henri Meschonnic

Day 353

In your opinion, what "makes the difference" in a poem?

I am at the beck and call of poetry.
—Antouin Artaud

Read the following statements on beginning a poem:

One who writes a poem writes it because the language prompts, or simply dictates, the next line. Beginning a poem, the poet as a rule doesn't know the way it's going to come out, and at times he is very surprised by the way it turns out, since often it turns out better than he expected, often his thought carries further than he reckoned.

—Joseph Brodsky

Usually I begin a poem with an image or phrase; if you follow trustfully, it's surprising how far an image can lead. Once in a great while I've seen the shape of the whole poem (never a very long one, though) and tried simply to follow the stages of plot, or argument.

—James Merrill

One of the ways in which I begin a poem is to accumulate a certain number of lines, phrases, images, and then pick out a few and ask myself, "How can I relate to these?"

—Reginald Shepherd

I never know what I'm writing about when I start a poem. Or almost never. There are very few poems where I actually know in advance what the poem will be and it does turn out to be that. But much, much more common is I simply feel some words, or I feel an image, and I listen. And a voice within me begins to speak. And it's only by following that voice that the poem then unfolds.

—Jane Hirshfield

And how about you? Which passage(s) resonate(s) the most with you?

Describe, in a poem, how you write a poem.

Write while the heat is in you . . .
—Henry David Thoreau

As you write . . .

Pay attention to your body, and to your
sensations. Are you tense, relaxed?
How do you breathe? Do you forget
about your body? Can you tell? How?

I would hope that my poems allow my readers to relish in the sounds of words.
—Bruce Weigl

Day 357

How about you?

Complete this line: "I would hope that my poems . . ."

A poem can be a bottle thrown out to sea, abandoned
with the hope that it will, someday, somewhere, turn
up on a beach, on the beach of the heart, perhaps.
—Paul Celan

Choose one of your poems and
throw it into the sea. Literally or sym-
bolically. For example, you could
make copies of one of your poems
and drop it into some mailboxes.

Day 358

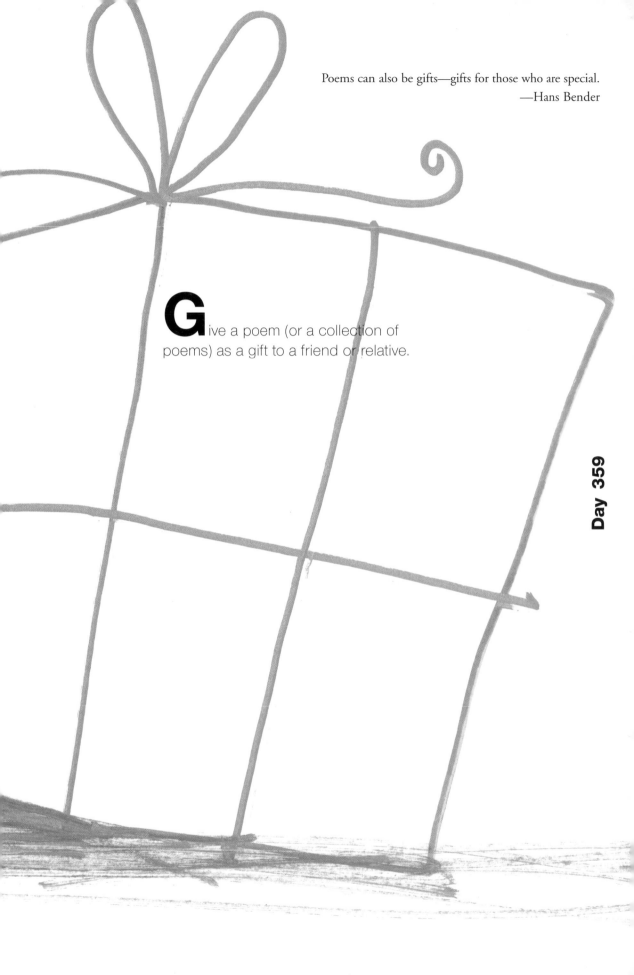

Poems can also be gifts—gifts for those who are special.
—Hans Bender

Give a poem (or a collection of poems) as a gift to a friend or relative.

Day 359

I don't look on poetry as closed works. I feel they're going on all the time in my head and I occasionally snip off a length.
—John Ashbery

Start a poem, but don't finish it. Keep it open-ended, so you can come back to it time and time again . . .

Write till your ink be dry, and with your tears /
Moist it again . . .
—William Shakespeare

Reread some of your poems. What are the words or themes that appear most often?

A poet's autobiography is his poetry. Anything else is just a footnote.
—Yevgeny Yevtushenko

Make a self-portrait composed of fragments of your poems.

Poetry is the universal language which the heart holds
with nature and itself.
—William Hazlitt

Reread the many definitions of
poetry included in this journal. Choose
the three (or five, or ten!) that seem the
most accurate to you.

Poetry is the revelation of a feeling that the poet
believes to be interior and personal [but] which the
reader recognizes as his own.
—Salvatore Quasimodo

Day 364

Aha! You turned this book around.
Now continue this movement, and write.

Yes, there is a Nirvanah; it is leading your sheep to a green pasture, and in putting your child to sleep, and in writing the last line of your poem.
—Kahlil Gibran

Gather the stars if you wish it so.
Gather the songs and keep them.
Gather the faces of women.
Gather for keeping years and years.
    And then . . .
Loosen your hands, let go and say good-by.
    Let the stars and songs go.
    Let the faces and years go.
    Loosen your hands and say good-by.
                —Carl Sandburg,
            "Stars, Songs, Faces"

Day 365

Can you say, by way of a poem, what it feels like to complete a poem?

Thank you to everyone who, through their advice, suggestions,
and encouragement helped me in the writing of this book.
Especially:
Candice Leduc and her students at Poligny Middle School,
who "tested" numerous activities in the journal,
and Annemarie Kordecki, pitiless reader!

In the same series

The Aspiring Writer's Journal
By Susie Morgenstern
Illustrations by Theresa Bronn

The Aspiring Artist's Journal
By Claude Lapointe
Illustrations by Sylvette Guindolet

The Library of Congress has catalogued this book under
Library of Congress Control Number 2007940073.
ISBN: 978-0-8109-7238-4

Copyright © 2007 Éditions de la Martinière
English translation copyright © 2008 Harry N. Abrams, Inc.
Translation by Gita Dineshjoo
Additional poetry and text selection by Gita Dineshjoo and Elizabeth Smith
Book design by Valérie Gautier

Printed and bound in China
10 9 8 7 6 5 4 3 2 1

HNA ▮▮▯▯▯
harry n. abrams, inc.
a subsidiary of La Martinière Groupe

115 West 18th Street
New York, NY 10011
www.hnabooks.com